MORE
THAN
A
DOLL

HOW CREATING A SPORTS DOLL TURNED
INTO A FIGHT TO END GENDER STEREOTYPES

JODI BONDI NORGAARD

Post Hill
PRESS

A POST HILL PRESS BOOK
ISBN: 979-8-88845-640-8
ISBN (eBook): 979-8-88845-641-5

Post Hill Press
New York • Nashville
posthillpress.com

Published in the United States of America
2 3 4 5 6 7 8 9 10

To my daughter Grace, the original Go! Go! Sports Girl, and my sons Peter and Ben, thank you for inspiring me every day since the day you were born. To my loving, smart, and patient husband, Steve, thank you for believing in me and equality. To my good friend and editor, Kara, thank you for telling me never to give up because girls deserve more. And to all the strong, smart, brave, and fierce women and girls, stay strong, hold hands, rise together, and create change.

TABLE OF CONTENTS

PART 3
DREAM BIG, GO FOR IT, AND DON'T GIVE UP

PART 4
THIS FIGHT IS STILL NOT OVER

INTRODUCTION

"Girls who play sports don't play with dolls."

"Girl empowerment was a trend a few
years ago. It's not anymore."

"You need to add more blonde, blue-eyed
dolls and make their legs longer."

"Generally, kids who are active don't read."

"A sports doll will never sell because girls like
fashion. Can you create a fashion doll?"

"Black dolls don't sell well."

"Boys don't read books about girls."

"I love your product, but it'll never sell
because it's not mainstream. It's not a
fashion doll, and girls like fashion."

Do you actually believe any of these statements? Of course not. But these comments are real feedback I received from toy industry and publishing professionals over the last decade in response to the Go! Go! Sports Girls dolls and books, the girl-empowerment brand I created and sold worldwide.

People continue to be averse to change that empowers women and girls. We talk a good talk about the importance of girl empowerment but cower when it comes to implementation. I know this firsthand.

Recently in an interview, I was asked, "Explain empowerment. By empowering women and girls, what is your goal?"

"Equality," I answered. "Empowering women and girls leads to confidence to create change. Women and girls feel empowered when they participate in sports. Sports have the power to create change."

While it's true more and more girls are participating in sports, they are also dropping out at increasing numbers between the ages of twelve and thirteen—the very time when girls need every ounce of their confidence and empowerment to take hold—to grow into women who know their full value and expect nothing less.

How can a sports doll change that trajectory? Why a line of dolls built in specification to a real girl's body, dressed to play eleven sports, with a companion book series that promotes social-emotional growth through sport with a female protagonist?

Because gender stereotyping begins at birth and becomes ingrained in societal expectations before children leave preschool. Gender stereotypes portray different and hierarchical gender roles assigned to women and men as natural and normal. They are more destructive than our culture perceives and, in fact, stand in the way of gender equality.

Dolls are still considered the primary toy for girls ages seven years and under, yet there are few choices beyond baby dolls and fashion dolls. Worse still are the sexualized fashion dolls that (still!) permeate toy shelves.

I have been challenging the toy industry for more than a decade to offer young girls something else, something that represents who they are now and how they are living in this moment of their little lives to give them the validation they need.

If one in three girls begins playing a sport by age six, and the global youth sports market is so big it is projected to grow from $37.5 billion in 2022 to $69.4 billion in 2030,[1] then why *shouldn't* she have toys and books that reflect her life and confirm her choices? If a young girl feels supported as an athlete—not just from her parents and coaches, but also from the toys she plays with and the books she reads—will she be more likely to stay in sport longer? To hold on to that unabashed confidence? To believe in herself and all she can accomplish?

Sure, society tells girls they can be strong, capable athletes—but hands them a doll that looks like she's dressed for the catwalk (or worse). And then we wonder why girls drop out of sports in droves when they enter puberty. Gender stereotyping begins early and in ways that are so evasive we fail to see the harm. "It's just a toy," after all.

Throughout this book, I connect the dots from sexualized dolls to the subtle damage inflicted on girls' confidence, to implicit biases we hold about gender, to decisions we make as adults that prevent true gender equity. I point out deeply rooted gender stereotypes in our culture in hopes to educate, make aware, offer suggestions, and accelerate progress for women and girls.

---

1   Market N Research (Global Youth Sports Market, February 13, 2023).

As I do this, I share my own story to illustrate how sexism and our patriarchal culture continue to be a pervasive problem in my fight to not only elevate girls but also dismantle gender stereotypes in the toy industry—a place that has great control over setting up girls' first perceptions of themselves.

I haven't come across a single person who disagrees with me: Girls play sports.

So why shouldn't their dolls?

PART 1

How Creating a New
Sports Doll Turned
into a Fight for
Women and Girls

CHAPTER 1

EQUAL PLAY?

"Women have always led. Even when they've been
denied official positions of power, they've
still fought for a better future."
— *Michelle Obama*

In 2021, The Toy Foundation, the philanthropic arm of
The Toy Association, a business trade association representing companies involved in youth entertainment, hired
the Geena Davis Institute on Gender in Media to conduct
a study on whether gender norms are reinforced in toys
and toy advertising and marketing.

The thirty-three-page report titled *Equal Play? Analyzing
Gender Stereotypes, Diversity, and Inclusion in Advertising and
Marketing for the Most Popular Toys of 2022* was completed
in June 2022.

Sounds like progress, right? But The Toy Foundation
didn't release the report to the industry or public when
they received the results. As someone who had worked on
behalf of The Toy Foundation to commission the study, I
knew something was wrong and so did the Geena Davis
Institute because my contact there said, "We have never
had an organization pay us for a study and not release it
the next day."

In January 2023, on a video meeting, I asked the lead person on the project from The Toy Foundation when they planned to release the report.

"The Toy Association Board of Directors decided not to move forward with the report. It won't be released," she said with a hint of embarrassment. She was the messenger, not the decision maker.

At the time, The Toy Association Board consisted of sixteen people: eleven men, only five of which were under age fifty, and ZERO people of color. If there is no diversity in leadership, there is a slim chance there will be diversity and inclusion throughout the industry, including the final product they put on store shelves.

Despite this lack of diversity, why shouldn't we expect older, white men to be a voice for change? Part of The Toy Association's mission is to champion the benefits of play by offering "expert advice on how toys and play can help kids build confidence, creativity, critical thinking, and other skills that will serve them throughout their lives." These board leaders had an opportunity to increase awareness about the harm gender stereotypes cause and be a catalyst for change.

"What?" I asked, trying to pick my jaw off the ground. "They paid for the study. Why wouldn't they want to move forward with such important information?"

"The board feels the report shows the toy industry and some key players in a negative light," she responded.

She's not wrong. The report clearly points to blatant stereotyping in the toy industry and by key players—the same major toy brands that fund The Toy Association. For me personally, this wasn't a surprise. That obvious stereotyping is why I started the Go! Go! Sports Girls dolls. The surprise for me was that even with hard data to back up what we knew was anecdotal information, The Toy Association wasn't willing to publicize the problem; they don't want to rock the money boat at the expense of doing what's best for our kids.

I want you to understand my motivation for sticking to my mission—why, despite all of the setbacks you will soon read about, I didn't give up. It's here in this report, so here's a summary of *Equal Play? Analyzing Gender Stereotypes, Diversity, and Inclusion in Advertising and Marketing for the Most Popular Toys of 2022.*

> The report confirms toys aren't just for fun. Toys and games help children develop cognitively and impart a broad range of social, emotional, and physical skills. But children's toys have been coded in ways that clearly convey expectations about distinctive male and female interests, tastes, and preferences, and they are even segregated into separate and clearly identifiable aisles in toy stores.

> It confirms that despite experts' calls for more gender-inclusive play, as well as parents' interest in expanded toy options, contemporary toy advertisements and toy products have not evolved much over time in terms of the social messages they convey about gender. While 2022 toy advertisements showed girls and boys playing with a variety of toys, most toys had clearly gendered associations with dolls targeted toward girls, but sports equip-

ment, cars, and toy weapons targeted toward boys. Marketing also continues to forge gendered associations in more subtle ways such as through color, music, narrator gender, and the selective use of imaginative (for girls) and aggressive (for boys) language. Portrayals of toys in this manner reinforce stereotypes about girls' and boys' interests and contribute to ideas that can hinder children's creativity and ambition.

It confirms that representation matters. Toys are learning tools that communicate to children how they should move through the world, what opportunities are available, and what kinds of things they might aspire to. But if toy advertisements send messages that girls should be calm, nurturing, and beautiful while boys should be strong, aggressive, and competitive, then such advertising reinforces rigid, unhelpful gender norms. And if children of color and differently-abled children are barely being spoken to or represented at all, then these kids are rendered invisible. Toy advertising that features accurate and inclusive portrayals of all types of children can reduce negative stereotypes and can also help children to see themselves represented in ways that positively contribute to their cognitive development and sense of personal identity.

The gendering of toys communicates rigid social norms surrounding how girls and boys should behave. In turn, this buttresses an outdated gender binary, defining boys and girls in terms of what differentiates them rather than what similarities they share. Gender-inclusive products and marketing strategies for toys tend to be the exception rather than the rule.[1]

The toy industry needs to do better because a child's early experiences affect their development and life choices, which ultimately affects the composition of the workforce, economic strength, community leadership, political leadership, household equality, and overall gender equality.

Believing in gender equality begins with choices for creative play. As Anne Marie Kehoe, former Walmart vice president of toys, points out, "It's not that there isn't desire for change within the toy industry, but there isn't a blueprint yet."

This book marks the start of a new blueprint aimed at disrupting reliance on gender tropes and lazy stereotypes. The goal is to broaden diversity and inclusion and to give children choices that reflect and validate who they are and who they want to become.

---

1   "Equal Play? Analyzing Gender Stereotypes, Diversity, and Inclusion in Advertising and Marketing of Toys" (Geena Davis Institute, April 17, 2024), https://geenadavisinstitute.org/research/equal-play-analyzing-gender-stereotypes-diversity-and-inclusion-in-advertising-and-marketing-for-the-most-popular-toys-of-2022/.

CHAPTER 2

LOVELY LOLA IS NOT MY DAUGHTER

"To our daughters: You are powerful. You are limitless. You belong at every single table where decisions are being made."
— *Ayanna Pressley*

Some people have an "aha moment" in glamorous places—while summiting a mountain or walking alone at sunset on a deserted beach. Others find clarity while mediating or practicing mindfulness. Me? My moment of clarity? The time when I said, *I see a problem, there must be a better way, and I can be the one to fix it*…happened at a toy store. Not quite as glamorous, but it does go to show that inspiration lies in unexpected places.

Here's what happened that summer day in 2006. If you are a parent, you will be familiar with this scene: You are running into the toy store with your child because she needs a wrapped birthday gift for a party that she is attending in thirty minutes! That was me with my nine-year-old daughter, Grace. Her scrubbed face pink from exertion from soccer practice, hair in messy pigtails, shin guards still on, running behind me pointing out toys she liked. We were quickly moving through the aisles when a line of dolls grabbed my attention. They were dressed in belly-baring clothing, high heels and makeup. I picked up one of the dolls, and the name on the hangtag was "Lovely Lola." I started to pick up other dolls in the line, and there was "Dazzlin' Destiny," "Cute Candy," and "Sizzlin' Sue," to name a few.

I was out of my mind! I thought to myself, *What in the world are we marketing to girls? These dolls look like hookers!* At that moment, I knew there wasn't one parent who wanted their daughter to look, act, or be called "Lovely Lola," "Dazzlin' Destiny," "Cute Candy," or "Sizzlin' Sue."

I bought "Lovely Lola," while scolding the salespeople in the toy store as my daughter ran behind me asking, "Mom, is that the birthday gift for Maddie?" I said, "No, I am buying it to show Dad," which confused her even more.

This encounter with Lovely Lola crystallized something I already knew. Our culture, specifically the toy industry, was doing a lousy job providing girls with strong, smart, and powerful images. Maybe I couldn't change an entire culture, but there had to be something I could do.

What had preceded this moment of clarity were layers of personal experiences with gender inequality and gender stereotyping. Gender issues had been on my radar for years, for decades, but I didn't know what I could do personally to change it, so I pushed it aside…until I met Lola. Lovely Lola represented all that history in a fourteen-inch plush doll. And that's when I realized how I was going to deal with gender issues. Girls needed a doll that emphasized what girls' minds and bodies can do versus what their bodies look like.

My encounter with Lovely Lola was what organizational psychologist and *New York Times* best-selling author Adam Grant calls a *vuja de* moment. Vuja de is the reverse of déjà vu. "We face something familiar, but we see it with a fresh perspective that enables us to gain new insight from old problems," Grant writes. In his book *Originals: How Non-Conformists Move the World*, he discusses how it is our nature to "rationalize the status quo as legitimate" and points out that "originality is taking the road less traveled, championing a set of novel ideas that go against the grain but ultimately make things better."[1] Basically challenging the status quo.

My hero for challenging the status quo on gender equality is Billie Jean King. When I was nine-years-old—the same age as Grace when we discovered Lovely Lola—I fell in love with tennis and idolized Billie Jean King. It was the era of fierce female tennis players: Chris Evert, Martina Navratilova, Margaret Court, Virginia Wade, and Evonne Goolagong.

When I learned that Bobby Riggs, a fifty-five-year-old man I had never heard of, had challenged my idol, the number one female tennis player in the world, who was twenty-nine, I laughed and thought he was crazy. It didn't matter that, thirty years prior, he was one of the world's top tennis players. For weeks I looked forward to the "Battle of the Sexes," not realizing then one of its lasting memories would become my first exposure to sexism, chauvinism, and stereotyping all rolled up into one tennis

---

1   Adam Grant, *Originals: How Non-Conformists Move the World* (Penguin Books, February 7, 2017).

match—and not from the nutty pomp and circumstance created by Riggs, but from my own father.

Excited for the big day, I sat on the gold shag carpet in front of our living room TV and watched the circus-like procession as Bobby Riggs and Billie Jean King entered the Astrodome in Houston on September 20, 1973. My dad, also a big tennis fan, joined me. My dad was a great athlete, and I shared his love for sports—at least most sports. He was kind, gentle, and sweet, so when he sat next to me on our striped velvet gold chair to watch Billie versus Bobby, I was thrilled and said, "Dad, I can't wait to watch this match and see Billie kick Bobby's butt."

"Billie's not going to win," he said. "There is no way a woman can beat a man." I didn't understand. He lived in a household of a fierce woman and girls. His response infuriated me and may have set up the trajectory of my life.

"You're wrong," I said, fuming. "Not possibly wrong, but 100 percent dead wrong!" For the rest of the match, I sat in front of his chair seething while I rooted for Billie. I hadn't anticipated the "Battle of the Sexes" would turn into a battle between my dad and me

Billie won the first two sets to my father's disbelief, but he chuckled and said, "Bobby is going to turn it on now." I stood my ground and kept my faith in Billie.

Bobby never recovered, and Billie won the third set. She became the champion of the "Battle of the Sexes." My dad kept saying, "I can't believe this," and I kept saying, "See, Dad, I told you so. Women CAN beat men at tennis." I felt as triumphant as Billie Jean and skipped out the door, tennis racket in hand.

To this day, the game remains the most-watched tennis match ever. Years later I learned that Billie Jean King viewed the match as more than a publicity stunt, but something important both for women's tennis and for the women's movement as a whole. She said, "I thought it would set us back fifty years if I didn't win that match. It would ruin the women's tour and affect all women's self-esteem."[2] Today, I still admire Billie, but now it's because of her overall fierceness and dedication to the advancement of women.

That gender-role breaking match took place the year after she fought tirelessly and courageously for Title IX. The civil rights law that prohibits sex discrimination in all federally funded school programs, including sports, passed on June 23, 1972. The law opened doors and removed barriers for girls and women. I was one of those girls. I went on to play tennis and run track in high school, where prior to Title IX, these sports weren't always offered. Since Title IX's passage, female participation at the high school level has grown by 1,057 percent and by 614 percent at the college level. Sadly, Title IX remains the only law that grants women any kind of equality in America.[3]

There is a misconception that the Equal Rights Amendment protects women, but the ERA has never been added to the Constitution. The amendment states: "Equality of rights under the law shall not be denied or abridged by the United States or by any state on account

---

2 Larry Schwartz, "Billie Jean Won for All Women," http://www.espn.com/sportscentury/features/00016060.html.

3 Billie Jean King Enterprises, https://www.billiejeanking.com/equality/title-ix/.

of sex." "This simple, 24-word amendment is packed with the potential to protect access to abortion care nationwide, defeat bans on gender-affirming healthcare, shore up marriage equality, eliminate the gender wage gap, help end the epidemic of violence against women and girls and so much more," said Rep. Cori Bush (D-Mo.). "With the flick of a pen, we can cement constitutional gender equality as the law of the land." Unfortunately, our lawmakers have failed women over the last 100 years in their failure to pass the ERA, which was first introduced in 1923.

Despite my dad's attitude toward the "Battle of the Sexes" match, he has always supported me and told me a thousand times how proud he is of me. That's why, at nine-years-old, I was so confused when he didn't believe Billie Jean King could beat Bobby Riggs. I took it personally. If he didn't believe a woman could beat a man, how could he still believe in me?

I have seen throughout my life men supporting and wanting the best for their daughters, sisters, mothers, wives, and the women near and dear to them, but I've come to understand that there is a deeply rooted cultural undercurrent that goes unnoticed: men support women close to them, but when it comes to overall gender equality, there isn't the same whole-hearted belief in women's strength, ability, or worthiness of equality. That deeply rooted cultural undercurrent makes it easy for a male toy executive to justify creating a line of sexualized dolls for young girls.

That's the status quo I wanted to shake up. As I was holding Lovely Lola, I could see the potential for a doll that mirrored all the confidence little girls embody before the world tells them otherwise, and they begin to hold back out of self-consciousness. I wanted to give girls a doll that validated their strength and self-assuredness, so they could stay true to their strong bodies and smart minds. I wanted a doll for my daughter that reflected who she was—a girl who played sports.

In my naiveté I believed creating a doll that broke gender stereotypes would be the sweet, happy ending to my own story of bucking up against gender inequity. Instead—no matter how well the dolls were received by media, or the number of awards they won, or their success on the shelves of the world's largest retailer—the Go! Go! Sports Girls became the beginning of a whole new battle. This time, however, I wasn't fighting for myself. I am in this on behalf of all girls who deserve better—not only from the toy industry, but also from our culture.

CHAPTER 3

CREATING CHOICE IN THE TOY AISLE

"To bring change you must not be afraid to take the
first step. We will fail when we fail to try."
— *Rosa Parks*

After my vuja de moment in the toy store and buying
Lovely Lola, I showed the scantily dressed doll to my
husband Steve. In addition to Grace, we have an older
son Peter and a younger son Ben. I didn't want my sons to
grow up accepting a sexualized doll as the norm any more
than I did my daughter. I was fired up and told Steve I
could do something better. I could create a positive-imaged doll that encourages girls to be healthy physically,
mentally, and emotionally through sports and physical
activity. A doll that focuses on healthy and active play
over beauty and body image. After hearing all my ideas
over the years (more on that later) and not always enthusiastically embracing them, he agreed this was a good one.

I ran the concept by my closest friends who I knew
would give me honest feedback, and unironically all our
discussions took place while exercising or playing a sport.
Brenda and I talked on our runs; Sarah and Amy while
on the chairlifts when skiing; Renee on bike rides; Deb

while swimming; Steph, Roxanne, and Molly on walks; and Erica and Emily while playing golf. My friends and I were living examples of girls who grew up being active and loving sports. And now we were also moms who often felt we were swimming upstream trying to provide healthy choices for our kids.

That was also part of my motivation in 2005 for starting a Girls on the Run chapter in Glen Ellyn, Illinois. I was a coach for four years, and Grace participated for three years. Running and exercise helped me be a better mom, wife, friend, and helped me show up for myself in better ways: I was more patient and productive. Exercise clears my head and has always been my meditation. Through Girls on the Run, I had the opportunity to inspire girls to be healthy and confident while creatively integrating running. And participating in this program catalyzed my mounting sentiments around gender disparities into action. Through my experience as a coach and later as a board member in Chicago, I got a taste of how it felt working on behalf of equality, and I was committed and passionate about it.

While my main reason for creating the Go! Go! Sports Girls was to offer a product void of the negative and sexy images marketed to girls, I was also concerned about the rise in childhood obesity. In 2006, nearly 17 percent of children (more than 12.5 million) were overweight, and this number was steadily rising.[1]

---

1   "NCHS Pressroom - 2006 Fact Sheet - Obesity Still a Major Problem" (Centers for Disease Control and Prevention, February 12, 2007), https://www.cdc.gov/nchs/pressroom/06facts/obesity03_04.htm.

I have always believed in healthy eating and the benefits of fueling your body with nutritious foods and passed this belief to my three now adult children. However, we often argued when I was the "snack mom" for their sports teams. They told me I was a terrible "snack mom" because I brought cut fruit and water for the team and their siblings while other parents brought Gatorade and packs of cookies. I have never in my life craved anything sugary after exercising and knew this was not a habit that should be created at a young age. I was adamant about fueling their little bodies with healthy food.

There were some Saturdays, after three soccer games, my kids were each given three Gatorades containing a whopping 34 grams of sugar each, so they were offered a total of 102 grams of sugar by noon *just in their drinks*. The American Heart Association recommends 25 grams of sugar per day for children.[2] I had parents tell me to relax, that it was fun for the kids, and it wasn't a big deal. I never caved.

And I get it, parenting is hard. We cut corners to keep our sanity. Certainly, marketing campaigns justify those uneasy moments when we want to do better by our children. If something is on the market, shouldn't we assume it's safe? What's the harm in the grand scheme of their lives? How can a seemingly minor choice at such a young age leave an impression on their adult lives? We can easily dismiss the link of after-soccer sugary drinks on future diabetes as easily as we can dismiss the link between

---

2   American Heart Association, Sugar Recommendation Healthy Kids and Teens Infographic. https://nutritionsource.hsph.harvard.edu/2016/08/23/aha-added-sugar-limits-children/

playing with a sexualized doll on self-imposed limits for a future career.

What I saw in my doll concept was not only a doll that represented girls as they are but also had aspirational qualities to encourage healthy choices. Kids were beginning to sit in front of screens at longer and longer intervals at the expense of active play. Dona Matthews, PhD, co-author of *Beyond Intelligence: Secrets for Raising Happily Productive Kids*, writes, "Play is not only important for physical development and as a way to have fun, but play builds children's brains, and gives them the tools they need for coping and resilience in a rapidly changing world."[3]

So why not creative play that encourages and celebrates physical activity? Physical activity is associated with improved academic achievement, healthy body image, reduced stress, better sleeping habits, and positive effects in self-esteem, goal setting, and leadership. The benefits extend into adulthood. Adolescents who play sports are eight times as likely to be active at age twenty-four as adolescents who do not play sports.[4] According to research conducted by Ernst & Young, 94 percent of women who hold C-suite level positions are former athletes.[5]

---

3   Dona Matthews, "Say Yes to Play" (Psychology Today, August 25, 2018), https://www.psychologytoday.com/us/blog/going-beyond-intelligence/201808/say-yes-play.

4   "Youth Sports Facts: Benefits" (Project Play, n.d.), https://project-play.org/youth-sports/facts/benefits.

5   Rebecca Hinds, "The 1 Trait 94 Percent of C-Suite Women Share (and How to Get It) | Inc.Com" (Inc., February 8, 2018), https://www.inc.com/rebecca-hinds/the-1-trait-94-percent-of-c-suite-women-share-and-how-to-get-it.html.

The more I studied the problem, the more resolved I became: Girls play sports, and so should their dolls.

Moving forward, I had a lot I needed to figure out. I knew nothing about the toy industry, product designing, manufacturing, shipping, bringing a product to market, or where I was going to store everything, but I was determined to learn. First, I needed to find out if there were any sports dolls already on the market.

CHAPTER 4

DEEP DIVE INTO THE WORLD OF DOLLS

"Be the change you wish to see in the world."
— *Gandhi*

The first doll I remember having—the one I couldn't live or sleep without—was a Drowsy Doll, a fourteen-inch talking doll with a pull cord that would say, "Mommy, kiss me goodnight," "I'm sleepy," or "I want a drink of water." The doll had a vinyl head and a soft body stuffed with tiny little beads. Every so often, after the doll had been loved and worn, the beads would start to leak all over the house. My parents would whisk my precious Drowsy Doll into the "hospital" for minor surgery. I remember waiting patiently outside the bathroom door until my dad appeared with my repaired Drowsy Doll.

Baby dolls that kids can feed and burp and bathe, and flimsy cute rag dolls, are considered a staple toy, but the next step in the doll category is a "fashion doll." Fashion dolls are dressed to represent current trends. They've been around since the mid-1800s—dolls with porcelain faces and hands, dressed to emulate grown women in fancy gowns with accessories such as hats, parasols, and gloves.[1] But many of today's fashion dolls aren't wearing clothes I've ever worn, nor would I want my daughter to wear. I believe these dolls deserve their own category—"sexy dolls"—because an overwhelming number of them aren't just scantily clad, they are marketed in suggestive ways, too.

Lovely Lola, Dazzlin' Destiny, Cute Candy, and Sizzlin' Sue, and a few of their other friends, Sassy Star, Rockin' Ruby, Punky Penny, and Oo-LaLa Olivia are part of Ty Girlz manufactured by Ty Inc., the creator of Beanie Babies. My kids loved Beanie Babies. Legs the Frog, Squealer the Pig, and Chocolate the Moose were childhood favorites, and today they still sit in their rooms. The Beanie Babies phenomenon is cited as elevating Ty Inc. CEO, Ty Warner, to billionaire status. I thought highly of Ty Inc. until the release of Ty Girlz.

I personally saw Ty Inc. in action at Toy Fair in 2009. Toy Fair is a trade-only event in New York City attended by retailers, distributors, wholesalers and not open to the public. It's lively, exciting, full of high energy, and an absolute blast. Many manufacturers hire talent to walk the 760,000 square feet of exhibition space at the Jacob Javits Convention Center dressed as characters in their line. I have seen (and taken pictures with) sixteen-foot Transformers, Paw Patrol, Peppa Pig, dinosaurs from Jurassic World, and Darth Vader.

The talk of the Toy Fair in 2009 was Ty Inc. They hired women to walk the aisles dressed in cropped tops,

---

1 "History of Fashion Dolls" (Fashion Dolls History - Types and Facts, n.d.), http://www.historyofdolls.com/doll-history/history-of-fashion-dolls/.

short skirts, and high heels with purple, yellow, and pink colored wigs and lots of makeup. They were dressed just like the Ty Girlz, and they looked like they were there to proposition sex, not sell dolls. It was awkward and uncomfortable, and many people were put off. Still, I was surprised by how many buyers swarmed their booth with interest. Coming off the Beanie Babies success, I figured buyers thought Ty Girlz were the next big hit and the next Beanie Babies phenomenon.

Bratz is another doll line that screams sexy. The brand name alone is bad enough. Manufactured by MGA Entertainment, Bratz dolls have over-sized heads, pouty lips, big eyes with cat-eye liner, icy eye shadow, extra-long eyelashes, tiny noses, hot pants, cropped tops, and removable feet. That's right, *removable feet*. Who thought that was a good idea? They look so emaciated that the American Psychological Association raised concerns over the body image that Bratz dolls allegedly promoted. They cited concern over the adult-like sexuality the Bratz dolls allegedly portrayed. Bratz defended the doll line by saying that the focus on the dolls was not on sexualization and that friendship was a key focus of the Bratz dolls.[2] Give me a break!

And then there is Barbie, a doll modeled after a racy German doll called Lilli that was inspired by the title character in a Playboy-style comic strip marketed to men. She worked as a secretary and was usually barely dressed. The slogan was, "Gentlemen prefer Lilli." Ruth Handler, who co-founded Mattel with her husband in 1945, put Mattel

---

2   "Bratz" (Wikipedia, June 4, 2024), https://en.wikipedia.org/wiki/Bratz.

designer Jack Ryan in charge of creating an American Lilli to market to girls. Handler's husband declared that she was "anatomically perfect."[3] Mattel introduced its doll as Barbie, Teen-Age Fashion Model.

For the last six decades, Barbie has dominated not only the toy industry but also infiltrated our culture with unrealistic body proportions. In a report by the Women's Sports Foundation, girls between ages five and eight who played with a Barbie doll reported lower body esteem and a greater desire to be thinner compared with girls who played with a doll that had more realistic body proportions. According to one estimate, only .001 percent of women match Barbie's large-breasted, narrow-hipped physical proportions.[4]

My sister Karen and I had an impressive collection of Barbie products; Malibu Barbie Dreamhouse, Barbie Beach Bus, swimming pool, dune buggy, washer and dryer, and dozens of Barbies and her friends. While Barbie has been an influencer of young girls for decades, portraying an image and lifestyle of beauty, my sister and I imagined our future selves differently. We would play with the collection from time to time, but we quickly became bored. We often came up with our own rebellious plans for the dolls. Once Karen snuck into our kitchen, strategically avoiding our mother, to collect food coloring,

3   Jill Lepore, "When Barbie Went to War with Bratz" (The New Yorker, January 15, 2018), https://www.newyorker.com/magazine/2018/01/22/when-barbie-went-to-war-with-bratz.

4   EJ Staurowsky et al., rep., *Her Life Depends On It II Sport, Physical Activity, and the Health and Well-Being of American Girls and Women* (Women's Sports Foundation, December 2009), https://files.eric.ed.gov/fulltext/ED515841.pdf.

scissors, permanent markers, and matches. We cut and dyed their hair and gave them tattoos. We saved one doll for a special experiment: to watch how quickly Barbie's hair would catch fire. The hair, by the way, was highly combustible. Her head began to melt, and the smell was awful…which tipped off our mother.

Our collection also included Barbie's younger and controversial younger sister, Skipper, created by Mattel to counteract the sex-symbol criticism of Barbie. Skipper was sporty and younger than Barbie, designed to be eight years old. But of course, Skipper couldn't simply be an innocent little girl without some form of sexualization. Mattel thought it would be a good idea for Skipper to go through puberty. When you rotated her arm one way, she would grow breasts; when you rotated back, the breasts would go away. Such terrific fun for girls. But why didn't they do the same for Ken? Can you imagine? Rotate his foot and watch his testicles descend!

Barbie and Skipper seem pretty innocent compared to Ty Girlz and Bratz dolls, but in 2014 I felt they tipped their position from fashion doll to sexy doll when Barbie, who was fifty-five years old, made the cover of the *Sports Illustrated* Fiftieth Anniversary swimsuit issue. As Mattel put it: "As a legend herself, and under constant criticism about her body and how she looks, posing in the issue gives Barbie and her fellow legends an opportunity to own who they are, celebrate what they have done and be #unapologetic."

I was outraged for two reasons. Number one, Barbie is plastic, so it doesn't matter if she is twenty-five, fifty-five, or a hundred and fifty-five years old—she is going to look the same! And number two, and more importantly, the doll is marketed to girls who are five to eight years old, but she appears on the cover of a magazine marketed to grown men, whose entire issue was devoted to promoting women as sex objects.

Yet Ty Girlz, Bratz, and Barbie all claim to empower girls. Mattel ran a campaign in 2015, "When a girl plays with Barbie, she imagines everything she can become" — and promoted Doctor Barbie, who wears her stethoscope with stilettos, a miniskirt, and a white lab coat embroidered "Barbie" in pink thread. When my sister showed Doctor Barbie to a friend who is an actual doctor, she laughed and said, "I have never seen a doctor dressed like that. That is ridiculous and hilarious and not a good or true role model for girls." MGA Entertainment CEO Isaac Larian said about his Bratz doll line, "Now more than ever before, Bratz empowers girls. We have doctors, lawyers, journalists."[5] Make that sexy doctors, sexy lawyers, sexy journalists. Somehow in Larian's mind, and the minds of many toy executives, sexualized dolls empower girls.

There is a giant chasm between the real lives and aspirations of children and what the toy industry pushes on them. Just because a large toy company launches a new product doesn't make it a good product. Just because toy companies want you to believe their product is on-trend doesn't make it a good choice. So how is it we are coming to have such "choices" on toy shelves?

---

5   Jill Lepore, "When Barbie Went to War with Bratz," (The New Yorker, January 15, 2018), https://www.newyorker.com/magazine/2018/01/22/when-barbie-went-to-war-with-bratz.

Answering that question required a deeper analysis of our patriarchal society, how our culture treats girls, and an examination of the leadership in the toy industry. Ironically, the 2023 *Barbie* movie did all that and more. Filmmaker Greta Gerwig's blockbuster movie packaged patriarchy perfectly in a pink box tied with a pink bow. There are so many enjoyable quips that call out our culture's comfort level with patriarchy, including representation.

While the real Mattel board had five women on its eleven-member board of directors at the time the movie was released, only one woman was represented of the seven executive officers on their corporate website. White men overwhelmingly make up the C-suite in this industry, so the imaginations of little girls are owned by corporations that are led by men.

The programming starts early, and the impact is lifelong.

CHAPTER 5

RAISING "GOOD" GIRLS

"No wonder studies show that women's intellectual
self-esteem tends to go down as years of education
go up. We have been studying our own absence."
— *Gloria Steinem*

From my first memory to around age eleven, I knew I
was strong, smart, and brave. I knew this because I
was good at sports and beat all the boys in grade school in
the fifty- and one hundred-yard dashes, I loved science,
and I advocated for myself and others. I was quiet but
confident. I was a good student, well-behaved, liked by
my peers and teachers, a good athlete — in addition to tennis, I ran track and loved to swim. I was an overall leader.
I felt respected. I was the kid who sat with the new kid
at school during lunch because I was empathic and knew
it had to be so uncomfortable. I was the kid who teachers pulled aside to ask for help in making sure kids who
seemed left out during recess were included. I was the girl
who focused on what her mind and body could do. Then
everything changed.

Over time I became more aware of labels, gender
issues, stereotyping, inequality, discrepancies, and gender
roles that I began to question. I have always been a good
observer, but at a young age I didn't always feel comfort-

able articulating my observations and opinions for fear of confrontation or being told I was wrong (except when it came to my dad during the "Battle of the Sexes "tennis match). I often waited for others to express their opinions first. I generally tested the water. You know, I wanted to be a *good* girl.

I was twelve years old when I entered seventh grade in 1976 at Sandburg Junior High School in Elmhurst, Illinois, a suburb west of Chicago. I came from a nurturing grade school environment, and junior high seemed much bigger and scarier, but exciting. I was still confident, but like any other kid at this age, I was beginning to feel more awkward, self-conscious, and unsure of myself, which made me impressionable. Still, I was eager to learn, get involved, and step outside my comfort zone. I was ready for my new environment and challenge; at least I thought I was.

It was September, during the first month of school, when I first experienced gender stereotyping and harassment. I was in science class, and my teacher was discussing something that confused me, so I did what students are to do when they have a question: I raised my hand. After I spoke, my teacher chuckled, so I knew he didn't think my question was a good one.

"You're blonde, and that's why you asked that question," he said while pointing his finger at me.

The class exploded with laugher. My face turned bright red, and I was mortified. In so many words, my teacher called me a dumb blonde! All I wanted to do was find a way to quickly leave the room to escape the embarrassment and humiliation, but there was no out. I asked a simple question, and it was turned into an issue about my appearance.

I tried to shake it off and didn't tell anyone including my parents because I was embarrassed. I knew the teacher was wrong, but I also questioned myself and thought maybe I was being overly sensitive. I had heard from men and boys in my life that I am too sensitive, and I should toughen up...because it was "only a joke." I believe people say this when they've said or done something unkind and want you to believe it's really your problem. But when you're young, and you hear something often enough, you eventually consider the possibility that it may be true.

Unfortunately, a similar situation happened again later in the year. I was in math class and hesitantly raised my hand to ask a question. Again, the teacher didn't think my question was very good and said in front of the class, "You're blonde and pretty, so you can't have brains, too." Again, my classmates roared with laughter at my embarrassment and humiliation.

So many feelings and thoughts ran through my head in that moment. I had always focused on what my mind and body could do, and I was beginning to question that. Maybe it was true I couldn't also be smart or athletic. Was I being too sensitive again? Should I toughen up? Everyone was laughing, so it must have been a joke.

I understand that we all have difficult experiences and adversity that we must deal with and overcome during our childhood. I am not opposed to adversity or "character building," but these two teachers — these "leaders" — gave permission to my classmates to call me dumb based on my appearance. For the next two years, I was often referred to as the dumb blonde at the bus stop, in the lunchroom, or at social settings.

Then, at the end of my eighth-grade year, two male teachers in their thirties asked me to come to their classroom after school. By then I was exhausted and beat down with the dumb blonde jokes, and I never raised my hand again. I thought they wanted to discuss a project I was working on, a test, or my grades.

I will never forget the day, and I feel anxious as I write this. I was wearing peach bell-bottom pants with a button-down patterned, long-sleeved shirt tucked in when I entered the room. One teacher was sitting on top of his desk while the other was standing next to the desk. They said they wanted to tell me something, but they gave me a vibe that this something was going to make me uncomfortable. They kept looking at each other and chuckling.

They proceeded to tell me how hot I was and how lucky the boys were that I was about to enter high school. If I was supposed to feel flattered, their plan backfired.

I couldn't respond verbally, but my eyes grew wide from shock. My face flushed with embarrassment, and tears ran down my cheeks. To this day the memory makes me cringe. I know the response was not what they expected, but what *did* they expect? I get even more creeped out thinking about what their expectations were in exchange for what they clearly believed was a "compliment." I ended the conversation by running out of the room in a panic.

In 2017, a report by Girl Scouts showed more than one in six girls in elementary and secondary schools have dealt with gender-based harassment. As Dr. Andrea Bastiani

Archibald, Girl Scouts' Developmental Psychologist, explains, "Catcalling and other objectifying behaviors can make girls feel their value lies solely in how they look as opposed to what they think, or the things they can accomplish. That kicks off a domino effect of girls engaging in self-objectifying—feeling overly concerned about how they look, comparing their bodies to those of other girls and women, and even judging other girls based on their looks." Another study showed that many girls ages fourteen to eighteen have experienced unwanted kissing or touching—more than one in five.[1]

Those two teachers must have worried about the consequences of their actions because the following day—a day I dreaded going to school—a male administrator asked me to come to his office. I began to panic again. *What had I done wrong*, I wondered? He asked me if everything was okay and if there was anything I wanted to discuss or talk about. I didn't want to talk about it because I wanted the situation to go away.

In hindsight, I realize this was a mistake. I never told my parents, my sister, or my friends because I was embarrassed and feared no one would believe me, or I would be told I was overreacting.

For the next four years in high school, my goal was to slide under the radar and sit on the sidelines. I no longer raised my hand, participated in class, or tried my hardest for fear of standing out. I still participated in sports and

---

1   "One in Ten Girls Is Catcalled Before Her 11th Birthday. Here Are 6 Things Parents Can Do About It" (Girl Scouts, n.d.), https://www. girlscouts.org/en/raising-girls/happy-and-healthy/happy/stop-catcalling-girls-and-sexual-harassment.html.

student council, but I never chose to be captain or president because I decided I was best in a supporting role.

By my senior year in high school, I realized that tactic didn't serve me either. My guidance counselor told me I was "too nice" to go to college and into business, and I was better suited for a secretary position or assistant's position. What I viewed as my strengths at a younger age—my compassion, empathy, and kindness—were now considered weaknesses. I was told I was, "too sensitive," all of which reinforced my insecurities that had been created over the years. The flame of that strong, smart, and brave girl was now only a flicker. I didn't know then if the fire inside me would return; all I could manage was to keep the flame from burning out.

Now I look back and wonder what could have helped me then. I firmly believe if I was able to learn about the accomplishments of women in my studies—the way I learned about the many accomplishments of men— then maybe I could have deflected the harassment more confidently.

In high school, I remember dreading history class. It always frustrated me, and I never understood why I felt this way. I was often annoyed and thought, "here we go again" as my teacher showed photographs of famous white men and explained their great accomplishments. I realize now that history to me was just another reinforcement and reminder of this prevailing social phenomenon that women's contributions in society are not as important as men's contributions. Statements about women's achievements are often brief, and women are portrayed as supportive caretakers, so I didn't know where or how I could fit in.

According to a 2017 report by the National Women's History Museum, 89 percent of historical figures referenced in history books are men and when women are mentioned, 53 percent fall within the context of family and domestic roles. While there is an increasing public interest in motivating girls to embrace science, technology, engineering, and mathematics, social studies standards provide few historic examples of women or their achievements in these fields.[2]

As Jane Austen's character Anne Elliot says, "Men have had every advantage of us in telling their own story. Education has been theirs in so much higher a degree; the pen has been in their hands." History has been written about men, by men, so it's no mystery why women like me find it hard to connect.

According to David Sadker, co-author of *Still Failing at Fairness*, "One of the most effective ways in which dominant groups maintain their power is by depriving the people they dominate of the knowledge of their own history." It's hard not to feel frustrated and excluded when the Declaration of Independence states, "All men are created equal," and that masculine nouns and pronouns are the default in the English language.

Rosie Rios, the forty-third treasurer of the United States, decided to do something about the lack of women's

---

2   Elizabeth L. Maurer et al., rep., *National Women's History Museum* (2017), https://www.womenshistory.org/sites/default/files/museum-assets/document/2018-02/NWHM_Status-of-Women-in-State-Social-Studies-Standards_2-27-18.pdf.

history mentions and started Teachers Righting History, an educational project that highlights historic American women in classrooms across the country. Rios writes, "People value what they see every day, yet there are very few institutionalized practices that reinforce the critical role women have played in American history. Just like currency, recognizing historic figures who can serve as role models for future leaders may have an enormous impact on the aspirations for both girls and boys."[3]

While children often miss out on learning about the accomplishments and possibilities of women in school, they are also bombarded by messages through media channels, which reinforce sexualized stereotypes and social norms. Advertisements, television, social media, music, books, and film are present almost everywhere in current culture and often deliver confusing and con-flicting messages. But these messages hurt the most when delivered in person.

Amy Morin, author of *13 Things Mentally Strong Women Don't Do* writes, "In my seventh-grade algebra class, my teacher always asked a sports-related bonus question that had nothing to do with math. This bonus question had to do with a Major League Baseball player. Fortunately, I loved baseball, and I knew the answer. When the teacher gave me my test back, across the page in red ink were the words '0 points. You only got this right because one of your friends told you the answer.' He assumed I couldn't possibly know the answer to an obscure baseball question

---

3   Rosie Rios, "What Is Teachers Righting History" (Teachers Righting History, September 18, 2016), https://teachersrightinghistory.org/what-is-teachers-righting-history/.

unless I cheated. My dad the next day wrote a note to the teacher telling him, 'Amy knew the answer fair and square. But what's not fair is that you ask sports-related questions that have nothing to do with math. Clearly, you are trying to give the boys an advantage since most 13-year-old girls aren't following male professional sports that closely.' The next day in class, my teacher announced, 'I can't give you bonus questions anymore because someone's father thinks I'm sexist.' The teacher didn't see his wrongdoing but pushed the blame on Amy and her father.

Nicole LaVoi, Director of the Tucker Center for Research on Girls and Women in Sport at the University of Minnesota, said, "I've been an advocate and feminist for girls and women in sports since I was 10 -years-old. I tried out for the boy's travel basketball team and made the team. The principal called me into his office and tried to get me to quit by telling me that I was taking the spot of a boy and shouldn't I do ballet or Girl Scouts. Luckily, I had parents that empowered me to do what I wanted to do."

It's no wonder then that women and girls begin to suppress their ambition. Like the game of Whac-A-Mole, they get beaten down every time they start to rise.

A few years ago, a friend of mine took a position as the managing partner at a large law firm. She asked all the partners in the firm to write a short description of their job responsibilities. She told me they basically have the same job and responsibilities but different clients and in-house projects. She said she was shocked at the descriptions. Every male partner started his paragraph with "I lead," and every female partner started her paragraph with "I assist."

We can't be surprised at such results when girls grow up hearing that they need to be good, be nice, sit on the sidelines, and don't be loud. Being nurturing, compassionate, and empathetic is too often regarded as weak. But then, when these same girls grow up to be women, they are told to lean in, change who they are to fit in, toughen up, and get bombarded by self-help that says they can be fixed. Women and girls are not broken. It's our system that's broken and our culture that needs to be fixed.

CHAPTER 6

BRANDS FLAUNTING SEX APPEAL

"It's a whole system out there that's transmitting
these inequitable norms."
– *Kristin Mmari*

O ne of my first memories of confusing and conflicting
messaging in media was at the age of eleven. The
perfume rage in 1975 was Love's Baby Soft, a powdery
and light fragrance marketed to tween girls, which all my
girlfriends and I loved. It was sold everywhere, was inex-
pensive, and had a strange yet appealing baby smell, but
that's where the innocence ended. In the TV spot, a grown
woman is dressed in a youthful baby-doll dress holding an
over-sized lollipop to her lips with the tagline, "Because
innocence is sexier than you think." If that wasn't bad
enough, a creepy male voiceover says, "A cuddly, clean
baby…that grew up very sexy." The bewildering Love's
Baby Soft magazine ad pictures a very young girl made
up to look like a sexy adult holding a teddy bear with the
same disturbing tagline.

Jean Kilbourne, author of *So Sexy So Soon* and creator
of the *Killing Us Softly* film series, addresses the bizarre
Love's Baby Soft ad and commercial in her film. "She's

dressed to look like a little girl but she's a little girl with cleavage.... The fact that she's raising her skirt, that her legs are apart, that she's sucking on a lollipop, all of this is designed to give a very strong sexual message at the same time that it denies it, which is exactly what the product is telling you to do, to be both innocent and sexy at the same time. Now this kind of thing is of course insulting to adult women. What they're saying to us is don't mature, don't be grown up, don't be adult. I think it's also dangerous to little girls."[1]

This is a form of male gaze, an idea conceptualized in 1973 by feminist film theorist and professor of film and media studies at the University of London, Laura Mulvey, and is still prominent today in film, television, literature, and more. "The male gaze controls the narrative, which is that women are not equal actors in the world. Instead, their agency is reduced to that of an erotic or supporting object, with their value as a female form (and person) reduced to how it appeals to the male viewer and/ or to how threatening (or not) it is to the stereotypical male perspective. Likewise, this viewpoint also confines the male persona to their specific role as the protagonist, aggressor, sexual pursuer, and consumer of women."[2] The impact of male gaze is so deeply rooted in our culture, and it begins at an early age, that both men and women are not always aware of how it influences our choices and how we see ourselves and others.

1   *Killing Us Softly: Advertising's Image of Women*, film (Cambridge, Mass: Cambridge Documentary Films, 1979).

2   Sarah Vanbuskirk, "Understanding the Male Gaze and How It Objectifies Women" (Verywell Mind, May 14, 2024), https://www.verywellmind.com/what-is-the-male-gaze-5118422.

According to the 2007 Report of the American Psychological Association Task Force on the Sexualization of Girls, virtually every media form studied provides ample evidence of the sexualization of women, including television, music videos, music lyrics, movies, magazines, sports media, video games, the Internet, and advertising. This sexualization has negative consequences for girls and for the rest of society.[3]

In August 2015, the University of Alabama's Alpha Phi sorority was harshly criticized for a recruitment video that critics said objectified women. An outspoken critic and AL.com op-ed writer A.L. Bailey wrote, "No, it's not a slick Playboy Playmate or Girls Gone Wild video.... It's a parade of white girls and blonde hair dye, coordinated clothing, bikinis and daisy dukes, glitter and kisses, bouncing bodies, euphoric handholding and hugging, gratuitous booty shots, and matching aviator sunglasses. It's all so racially and aesthetically homogeneous and forced, so hyper-feminine, so reductive and objectifying, so Stepford Wives: College Edition. It's all so…unempowering." She went on to say, "This video has a clear sales pitch: beauty, sexuality, and a specific look above all. They're selling themselves on looks alone, as a commodity. Sadly, commodities don't tend to command much respect. So who is buying what they're selling?" Bailey asks.[4]

---

3   Eileen Zurbriggen et al., "Report of the APA Task Force on the Sexualization of Girls," (American Psychological Association, n.d.), https://www.apa.org/pi/women/programs/girls/report-full.pdf.

4   A.L. Bailey, "'Bama Sorority Video Worse for Women than Donald Trump" (AL.com, August 14, 2015), https://www.al.com/opinion/2015/08/bama_sorority_video_worse_for.html.

Mashable.com reported "the op-ed unleashed a fury of comments—with several even defending the video, calling it harmless fun—before the hate spread to YouTube and social media comments."[5] I wish I had been more vocal in defending these young women. It certainly wasn't harmless fun, and I didn't condone it, but I did see a disconnect between the girls' actions, social culture norms, and the critics. To answer Bailey's question, girls are buying what the manufacturers and retailers are selling. That's the problem.

These eighteen to twenty-one-year-old young women grew up with these images of Daisy Dukes, glitter and kisses, bouncing bodies in their media: all on TV, movies, music, music videos, books, magazines, social media, advertising, their clothing, and even toys. In the video, the young women imitate the behaviors they grew up seeing, reading, and hearing, and then we shame and criticize when they emulate them. We are slapping the wrong hands. We are slapping the small hands, and we need to start shaming and slapping the big hands of the manufacturers, retailers, publishers, marketers, advertisers, and studios who promote and sell sexy, socially inappropriate, and unattainable beauty images to girls.

Professor of psychology at Northwestern University and author of *Beauty Sick*, Renee Engeln, PhD writes, "We have created a culture that tells women the most important thing they can be is beautiful. Then we pummel them with a standard of beauty they will never meet. After that,

---

5   Neha Prakash, "University of Alabama Sorority Deletes Recruitment Video after Intense Backlash" (Mashable, March 11, 2022), https://mashable.com/archive/alabama-alpha-phi-recruitment-video.

when they worry about beauty, we call them superficial."[6] Critics need to start looking at the bigger picture before they start shaming women and girls.

Humans learn through observational and social learning; watching others and then imitating or modeling what they say or do. It is often used in advertising and marketing, and the hope is that viewers will imitate what they see. A 2012 study conducted by Chan, Ng, and Williams shows how adolescent girls pick up gender-specific stereotypes and behaviors from advertising and media. In their study, they show how young girls aspire to be much like the images they see.[7]

Let's connect the dots. Observational and social learning + girls picking up gender specific stereotypes + every media form providing evidence of the sexualization of women = University of Alabama's Alpha Phi sorority video! Why in the world are we shocked?

Sometimes it's not just the advertising that's sexist; it's the product. When my daughter was a pre-teen, the popular clothing store was Abercrombie & Fitch. I had many issues with this store: the potent cologne smell, the blaring music, the hyper-sexual marketing and clothing, and the sexualization of the young store associates. Grace and I had many conversations about my dislike and concerns about this iconic teen retailer, but in her eyes and the eyes

6   Renee Engeln and Teri Schnaubelt, *Beauty Sick: How the Cultural Obsession with Appearance Hurts Girls and Women (HarperCollins Publishers, 2017)*.

7   Kara Chan, Yu Leung Ng, and Russell B Williams, "Adolescent Girls' Interpretation of Sexuality Found in Media Images"(Hong Kong Baptist University, 2012), https://scholars.hkbu.edu.hk/ws/portal-files/portal/55362580/RO_coms_ja-13_JA026140.pdf.

of every pre-teen, this is what the "cool girls" wore. I will admit, I caved from time to time, and we shopped at the store, but there was a final moment.

Grace was being helped by a kind young female sales associate wearing Daisy Duke shorts, the extremely short, form-fitting, denim cut-offs, and I decided to look at the t-shirts for girls. I couldn't believe what I was seeing: t-shirts that read, "I'm not allowed to date unless you're hot," "I'd do your homework, but I don't even do mine," and "School is for catching up on sleep." At this same moment, Grace came out of the dressing room wearing Daisy Duke shorts. I immediately entered panic mode and quickly guided her back into the dressing room, explaining my anger with the store and not with her. I obviously was not the only parent who felt this way about the retailer. In 2016, Abercrombie & Fitch was voted the most-hated retail brand in the US according to the American Customer Satisfaction Index, but their popularity spanned for sixteen years.[8]

Around this same time, Grace needed a few bras. I wasn't sure where to take her, so we both decided on Victoria's Secret. I was never a fan of the lingerie brand, its "Angels" in their provocative ads, and the glitzy fashion shows, but together we went to a nearby store.

She felt uncomfortable walking into the store but quickly found the section she was looking for. I, on the other hand, was fixated on a floor-to-ceiling, ten-foot photograph of an overly thin woman with overly large breasts

---

8   Lucinda Shen, "This Is the Most Hated Retailer in the U.S." (Fortune, April 24, 2021), https://fortune.com/2016/02/25/this-is-the-most-hated-retailer-in-the-u-s/.

in red and black lace matching bra, garter belt, and under-wear, red high-heeled shoes, blonde hair blowing in the wind, and white, fluffy angel wings. She didn't look real. I pulled Grace over and explained to her that this was not the standard of beauty and that the woman in the ad was highly photoshopped, objectified, and sexualized.

She had heard my speech before, but I felt it was nec-essary to explain to her again that women shouldn't be valued for their physical appearance or what their body looks like, but women should be valued for what their minds and bodies CAN DO. I was unable to help myself, and I took it a bit too far according to Grace. While on my soap box, I pulled a few of the salespeople over to ask their opinion on the photograph and how it made them feel. Grace's face was red with embarrassment and said to me, "Mom, seriously? Sometimes you are so embarrass-ing." She was thirteen, and I understood her feelings, but I needed to be sure my daughter understood this unrealis-tic social cultural norm message sent by Victoria's Secret.

I kept watch on how images, products, clothing, toys, books, ads and more undermine women and girls and fuel gender stereotypes. Here are a small sample of some of the t-shirts I found marketed to girls and boys as young as five years old:

"ALLERGIC TO ALGEBRA"

"I'M TOO PRETTY TO DO MATH"

"MY BEST SUBJECTS: BOYS, SHOPPING, MUSIC, DANCING"

"I'M TOO PRETTY TO DO MY HOMEWORK
SO MY BROTHER HAS TO DO IT FOR ME"

"LADIES MAN"

"CHICKS ARE ALL OVER ME"

"SORRY LADIES I ONLY DATE MODELS"

It's hard to believe there are people who think these t-shirts for kids are funny, cute, or anything but demeaning, degrading, and irresponsible. These shirts and other products like them reinforce harmful stereotypes that tell boys their value and worth is dependent on the number of girls they conquer, and that tell girls their value and worth is in their appearance and to downplay their intelligence to make themselves more appealing to boys.

"This has a ripple effect that can harm boys as well as girls," says Christia Spears Brown, a University of Kentucky professor of psychology and author of *Parenting Beyond Pink and Blue: How to Raise Your Kids Free of Gender Stereotypes*. "It indirectly says that girls are only for sexual attention and not for friendship. Anything that says that only models are worthy of attention is never positive for girls." [9]

I also found insulting and overtly sexist t-shirts marketed to girls that read, "TRAINING TO BE BATMAN'S WIFE" and "I NEED A HERO." This tells girls that you can't be a superhero, but you can marry one, reinforcing they are the supporting character, in need of help or assis-

---

9   Beth Greenfield, "After Criticism, Forever 21 Pulls 'completely Inappropriate' Boys' t-Shirts from Website" (Yahoo!, July 12, 2016), https://www.yahoo.com/lifestyle/are-these-forever-21-boys-t-shirts-completely-inappropriate-213229687.html.

tance, their place is on the sidelines, and to cheer for their superhero. In comparison, similar t-shirts were marketed to boys, but they read, "TRAINING TO BE BATMAN" and "BE A HERO." A much different message telling boys they are the main character, brave, and girls need their help.

I found coloring books marketed to girls as *The Beautiful Girls' Colouring Book* and to boys, *The Brilliant Boys Colouring Book*. A GAP Kids ad referring to girls as the social butterfly and the boys as the little scholar. Young girls dressed in belly-baring clothing and makeup in ads for girl's clothing, toys, and yes, adult perfume. On their own these are all brief impressions, but collectively they have a big impact.

Peggy Orenstein, author of *Cinderella Ate My Daughter*, said, "I can't say one shirt, one Barbie doll...that one thing is not going to be a tipping point of making a difference, but it's the culture they grow up in that, of course, socializes them. There is such a large subset of messages that remind girls that they are not supposed to be assertive, or they're not supposed to be good at science or math or reinforce the idea that how you look is more important than who you are."[10]

One of these subsets can be seen through a 2021 study by the gender equality campaign Let Toys Be Toys. They analyzed over 300 ads to examine what they're telling kids about what it means to be a boy or girl, repeating their initial research done in 2015. While there has been slight

---

10   Jessica Samakow, "The Dangerous Lessons Kids Learn from Sexist T-Shirts" (HuffPost, December 7, 2017), https://www.huffpost.com/entry/dangerous-lessons-from-sexist-shirts_n_6102096.

improvement, stereotypes in toy ads are alive and kicking. "Key words used in ads featuring only girls focused on appearance and beauty (fashion, wear, style, stylist, glitter, glam, cool), consumerism (shop, mall), magic and fantasy (magic, magical), and relationships (love, cute, together, talk). The language in ads featuring only boys was dominated by themes of action (speed, activate, race, spin, flex) and conflict (battle, fight, smash, blast). Ads featuring both boys and girls together had a vocabulary covering a wider range of types of play and fun (game, fun, care, adventure, create, play, magic, make)." [11]

The media can also have a strong influence on adults too. A few years ago, my then seventy-six-year-old smart and confident mother-in-law returned from a trip overseas. She told me while waiting in an airport, she was browsing the magazine section in a bookstore and came across *W Magazine* with seventy-seven-year-old Jane Fonda on the cover. The caption read, "Jane Fonda Forever Activist, Sex Symbol, Legend," and her photograph was flawless. Her hair, eyes, skin, neck, white dress, and even her seventy-seven-year-old cleavage was flawless.

My mother-in-law told me it instantly made her feel insecure and question her own appearance because Fonda looked fifty-five-years-old. She wondered how that could be possible. I told her the photo was most likely airbrushed and retouched to erase wrinkles and alter body parts and ultimately change the reality of the photo.

---

11   "Who Gets to Play Now? – New Research on TV Toy Ads" (Let Toys Be Toys, August 4, 2023), https://www.lettoysbetoys.org.uk/tvads2021/.

She didn't buy the magazine to read the article, but Fonda discusses her career, men, fashion, and having plastic surgery. Our culture puts so much emphasis on the beauty of females from the day we are born to the day we die. It's no wonder girls at the age of eight lose self-confidence,[12] and women in their seventies continue to have their confidence eroded. Don't get me wrong: I admire Fonda for her work as an actress and political activist and growing old in the public eye cannot be easy…especially if you're a woman.

Media has tremendous power to influence girls, boys, women, and men, and how they define gender roles. With this power, corporations and media should be more responsible. Becoming an activist and advocating for that responsibility was a role I was unknowingly taking on when I created my line of sports dolls. What I didn't know then that I know now is that my dolls would never make it unless I forged a path of cultural acceptance for them first.

---

12   Claire Shipman, Katty Kay, and Jillellyn Riley, "The Confidence Gap for Girls: 5 Tips for Parents of Tween and Teen Girls" (The New York Times, October 1, 2018), https://www.nytimes.com/2018/10/01/well/family/confidence-gap-teen-girls-tips-parents.html.

CHAPTER 7

REPRESENTING GIRLS
AS THEY ARE

"The future belongs to those who believe
in the beauty of their dreams."
— *Eleanor Roosevelt*

In the summer of 2006 I searched high and low for other sports-themed dolls but didn't find any, except for a few Barbie "sports" dolls in high heels. I've never played sports wearing high heels, nor have I ever seen anyone play a sport wearing high heels, so thinking logically, they didn't qualify.

I saw a void in the market, and my optimism about my idea was growing. There were some seventy-five doll-brands on the market, the majority of which were fashion dolls. Dolls are in the top five most popular gifts for girls, and retail sales of dolls in the United States amount to more than three billion annually. I was convinced there was an opportunity and a need in the toy marketplace that represented the way girls really live, but I needed some hard facts and statistics to back up my beliefs.

According to the 2019 State of Play report released by the Aspen Institute, approximately 71 percent of children have played on a team or individual sport by the age of six. And of children six to twelve who play a regular sport, boys and girls show up in near equal numbers at 38 percent and 31 percent, respectively.[1]

It is estimated that 21.5 million kids between the ages of six and seventeen play team sports, but that number is far below the actual total because it doesn't count the millions of kids who start before age six. An estimated 47 percent of girls are already involved in at least one organized sport by age six. [2] Why the toy market was flooded with fashion dolls just didn't make sense.

Of course, anecdotally I knew plenty of girls who preferred sports over fashion. A few years ago, while keynote speaking at a Girls Empowerment Network event in Austin, Texas, I spoke to girls ranging from the ages of eight to fourteen. During my presentation, I did an informal survey and asked them if they had a free afternoon, what would they choose to do? They eagerly shouted out play with my friends, practice soccer, practice tennis, go to the pool, read, dance, draw, play with my dog, cook, ride my bike. Not one girl mentioned anything that had to do with fashion or their appearance. Girls have a variety of interests.

The Women's Sports Foundation had similar findings in their 2020 Keeping Girls in the Game report. It lists children's top favorite things to do, which includes organized and informal sports/athletics, hanging out with

1   Tom Farrey and Jon Solomon, rep., *2019 State of Play: Trend and Developments in Youth Sports (n.d)*.

2   Bruce Kelley and Carl Carchia, "Hey, Data Data--Swing!" (*ESPN*, July 11, 2013), *https://www.cbsd.org/cms/lib/PA01916442/Centricity/Domain/312/Youth%20Sports%20stats.pdf*.

friends, watching TV/movies/videos, playing outside, reading, dancing, art, singing, and many others, but no mention of fashion, beauty, or appearance.[3]

Convinced I was onto something, I began designing a sports doll. I named the line Go! Go! Sports Girls. I wanted the dolls to convey action and excitement. I found joy in playing sports, and I wanted that joy to come through in the name of the dolls.

I bought a large sketch pad and some fancy professional drawing pencils, hoping they would make me feel like an artist, which I'm not, and bring out some hidden, unknown talent. I had found a picture of Grace when she was about eighteen months old and began drawing character sketches of her. They were rough sketches, but they weren't too bad.

The sketch pad came with me everywhere I went, never knowing when inspiration would strike, or, as a mom of three, time would present itself. I remember being on a family trip to Wisconsin later that summer, sketching in the car while Ben napped, and Steve took the older two fishing. I used every free moment I had.

I wanted to make sure the body of the doll was in correct proportion to a little girl's body. My nine-year-old daughter and her friends were the perfect models. I measured the length of their legs, arms, torsos, and the size of their heads, and I shrunk everything down to create a properly proportioned doll. Years later, a toy buyer commented that the Go! Go! Sports Girls legs were too short,

---

3   "Keeping Girls in the Game: Factors That Influence Sport Participation" (2018).

and the torso was too long. My response was, "Because they are in correct proportion to a little girl's body!"

I was determined to give girls and their parents a positive-imaged option.

Grace was curious about my new project and decided to sketch alongside me, but she didn't sketch dolls, she drew their clothes. She and her good friend Mary-Claire (M.C.) decided to join forces to assist me in the doll creation, and they called their company MCG Strategy Co. They designed sports outfits, combined colors, named the dolls, and even wrote a marketing plan. They were my best consultants. I was impressed and proud of my young entrepreneurs.

They named each doll after friends and cousins and named one after themselves, too. Grace chose tennis, and M.C. chose dance, their favorite sports. The original Go! Go! Sports Girls came with hangtags that gave a little bit of information about each doll, and Grace and M.C. helped write all of them. For example, Tennis Girl, Gracie's read: "Gracie loves to hit winners! Her favorite shot is her backhand down the line. Before playing tennis, Gracie stretches, drinks plenty of water and eats a healthy snack for energy, like a banana. When she is off the court, Gracie likes reading and playing with her friends. Gracie likes to Dream Big and Go For It!"

Dancer Girl, M.C.'s read: "M.C. likes to move and groove! She likes to dance because it makes her feel free. She enjoys all types of dances, but Hip-Hop is her favorite. Before dancing she always stretches and eats a healthy snack, like strawberries. When she is not dancing, M.C.

likes playing the piano and practicing her cheerleading moves. M.C. likes to Dream Big and Go For It!"

I decided to name my company Dream Big Toy Company because my hope was to expand the line to embrace different interests. Peter and Ben often asked me when I was going to make a Go! Go! Sports Boys. In my concept, Dream Big Toy Company was like an umbrella and underneath it was the Go! Go! Sports Girls, but eventually my goal was to add Go! Go! Sports Boys, Go! Go! Reading Girl, Go! Go! Cooking Boy, Go! Go! Music Girl, Go! Go! Artist Boy. Humans are beautifully complex, and I wanted to offer empowering images and products, so girls and boys could play with multiple dolls that reflected their interests.

But to start, my mission was to inspire and empower girls through a brand that allowed them to "Dream Big and Go For It." My vision was to be the most sought-after brand that captures girls' lives as they are now: active, athletic, adventurous, and brave.

With my designs complete and my sketches for a prototype in hand, I was ready to take the next step, or, I should say, figure out what the next step should be. This wasn't the first time I had started a company, so I wasn't completely uncomfortable learning as I went along.

In 1991 I was working in sales for the Ritz-Carlton National Sales office in Chicago. My co-workers and I frequently sent gifts to clients, and one of the most popular gifts were gift baskets filled with gourmet foods and treats. One day while going through the uninspiring gift basket catalogs (this was before the World Wide Web and Google), I mentioned to one of my co-workers that I could create better and more unique gift baskets. In that moment I don't know that I seriously intended to launch a new career, but the idea—said aloud—stuck with me.

I began searching for potential products, attending gift shows, researching shipping options, and asking a lot of questions. While speaking with one woman about the possibility of including wine in my gift baskets, she asked, "Do you know Ina Pinkney? She has a wholesale bakery in Lincoln Park and occasionally sells gift baskets. You should talk to her. I'll let her know you'll be stopping by."

It was a crisp October morning as I walked from my apartment, taking notice of the fall colors on the tree-lined streets. I was brimming with enthusiasm for my next business venture. Even the soul-sucking discontent I felt with my current employment seemed to be dissolving away the more I imagined myself taking control of my future.

The smell from Ina's bakery caught my attention before I walked in unannounced. It wasn't a retail bakery but a wholesale and catering bakery, and towering baker's racks lined the room filled with her famous Blobbs, (a mounded cookie/brownie with three kinds of chocolate, walnuts, and pecans), cookies, muffins, and cakes. People dressed in white chef coats were busy creating, mixing, and baking. I felt like I had just walked into Willy Wonka's factory. A kind looking woman about twenty years my senior stood working at a table; it was Ina. I said hello, and she gave me a big smile before I could introduce myself.

"You're the one," she said.

I was caught off guard. "I'm the one what?"

"You have a kind smile. I can tell I like you, and you're the one."

She proceeded to tell me all about her gift basket business along with her bakery over coffee and a fresh baked muffin. She had plans to open a restaurant, which was why she was looking for the right person to take over the basket portion of her business. All she asked for was 5 percent of every sale over the next two years.

I left thinking, what just happened? This woman who I don't know wants to give me her business? I remember going to work that afternoon and telling my co-workers the story and saying, "Who does that?"

Well, Ina does that, and to this day she is a friend, mentor, and inspiration. She taught me to trust my instincts and showed me a level of honesty and kindness in business that I hadn't experienced before. There have been many moments in my career where I have referred back to Ina and her instincts and ask myself, what would Ina do? Ina eventually opened her breakfast restaurant called Ina's in the west loop and became a Chicago icon. She is often referred to as the "Breakfast Queen." I am proud to call her my friend.

I took a leap in faith, quit my job at Ritz-Carlton, and started my new business, Basket Expressions, in November 1991. Ina had a niche, and now I did too. All the gift baskets contained homemade baked goods and chocolates made by Ina and other women in the Chicagoland area. When I asked Ina about working with the other women, she said they were the best in the area, and it was important for women to support other women in business and in life. Ina was ahead of her time, and she was my hero. I had always supported women in life, and now as a female entrepreneur, I set out to support other women in business.

I rented space in a walk-out basement of a friend of Ina's in Lincoln Park, a neighborhood on the north side of Chicago, bought a few freezers for the perishable baked goods, and setup shop. The orders immediately started coming in…and then more and more and more orders. So many that I had to beg family members to help me fill all the holiday orders. It was exciting and exhausting, and I had a newfound appreciation for all entrepreneurs.

I realized quickly that my new basket business was seasonally heavy, so the following spring when I didn't have as many orders to fill, my goal was to bring in new business. I decided to call Harpo Studios, home to the Oprah Winfrey Show, to see if I could get an appointment with their human resource department. Why not? Why not me and my business? I believed in my product. And when you believe in your product, you know where your product belongs.

The call paid off; I secured a meeting to show them what I had to offer. I created a beautiful two-hundred-dol-lar gift basket filled with Blobbs, cookies, muffins, mini cakes, and chocolates. I gave a presentation to ten Harpo employees, mostly women, in one of Harpo Studio's con-ference rooms. It was a bit intimidating, but I knew I had a good product, and I gave it my best shot. I men-tioned that all the items in the basket were made by local women, which I knew was right up Oprah's alley. I left the basket for them to enjoy, and I left feeling less intim-idated and more confident. That afternoon orders from

Harpo Studios started coming in, and they became one of my biggest clients. I never had the opportunity to meet Oprah, but I signed her name a lot!

The word spread quickly, and on top of Ina's clients, I started to receive orders from companies and individuals throughout the country. I created baskets for corporate meetings for hundreds of people. I created individual baskets for birthdays, baby gifts, and special occasions. And around the holidays I hired ten people to help me create thousands of baskets.

Having succeeded as an entrepreneur before gave me the confidence to move forward with the Go! Go! Sports Girls. I didn't let not knowing a thing about the toy industry stop me.

CHAPTER 8

FROM PAPER TO PROTOTYPE

"Don't let anyone rob you of your imagination, your
creativity, or your curiosity. It's your place in the
world; it's your life. Go on and do all you can with it
and make it the life you want to live."
— *Mae Jemison*

By the fall of 2006, I started dissecting rag dolls. I was curious how they were made, what the stitching was like, what was used for the filling, hair, and fabric. My friend Jane was a seamstress who designed beautiful clothing for girls. I brought my drawings and dismembered dolls to her studio and asked if she would help me create patterns for the Go! Go! Sports Girls. She agreed.

Next, I needed to find someone who could create a doll prototype. This is not easy because there are special tools needed to make a doll due to the small pieces of fabric that are difficult to handle and maneuver in a sewing machine. Another friend of mine, Mary Ann, had a curtain sewing business and five young girls. I knew it was a long shot because she was busy with her business and young family, but I also thought my idea might resonate with her because of her daughters. I decided to reach out and ask if she would create the prototypes. She quickly declined explaining she had little time to breathe. I was disappointed but understood.

The next morning, Mary Ann called and said she had thought more about my doll idea, and while she had little time, she knew girls needed to see strong and positive images. She agreed to help.

As 2007 began, and for the rest of the year, Mary Ann and I worked together creating, trying, failing, and repeating until we came up with the correct prototype. I was also working with an embroider who was helping with the face details. Again, there was trial and error—the eyes were too far apart, the nose was too low, the color of thread was too blue or too pink. After nine months of learning and trying, we finally created a prototype I liked.

With the prototype in hand by 2008, I could start producing the Go! Go! Sports Girls, but I didn't know where. I went back to Jane for factory recommendations in Chicago. She used one and made the connection. The factory was a big warehouse in an industrial part of Chicago, and I met with the owner. I showed him the doll and he immediately chuckled, which wasn't a good feeling. He apologized and explained that if he were to make the doll, the cost would be around fifteen dollars per doll.

I did the math. If I paid fifteen dollars, then the wholesale price, which is generally a profit margin of 30 percent, would come to $19.50. The retailers must make a profit, which is usually double the wholesale price, would bring my suggested retail price to thirty-nine dollars. I knew there was no way a rag doll would sell for that amount. I needed to find another option.

I went back to Jane and asked about other factories in the US. She gave me two, one in Georgia and one in North Carolina. They had the same numbers as the guy in Chicago. I realized it was impossible to manufacture in the US with a competitive cost.

Fast forward to December 2016, when I was interviewed by CGTV (China Global Television Network) America on this topic. Donald Trump had just been elected president, and his most prominent campaign promise was to produce more goods in this country to keep manufacturing jobs in America. CGTV's question was, "Is this possible?" I said, sure, it's possible, but the Go! Go! Sports Girls Read & Plays (the doll and book sets that hit the market in 2014), would have to retail for at least fifty dollars to make a small profit, compared to $22.99 if manufactured in China.

After the interview, the reporters asked if they could bring a Read & Play to the Magnificent Mile, an upscale section of Chicago's Michigan Avenue filled with department stores and crowds of shoppers. Holding the Go! Go! Sports Girls Read & Plays, the reporters asked random people if they would be willing to pay fifty dollars for the doll and book set. The overall response was, *cute, but no way.*

I knew my best option to reach a competitive retail price was to manufacture in China but had no idea how. I explained my dilemma to my friend Lydia, who I have come to realize is a wealth of information and connections. She introduced me to a friend she had in the toy industry, Christy Kaskey, founder and creator of Kaskey Kids.

Christy became a great resource and friend and one of the kindest, most helpful and honest people I have ever met.

Christy referred me to the factory she used in Hong Kong as well as put me in touch with a representative from KB Toys, a large toy retail chain that eventually went out of business in 2009, who in turn referred me to two additional factories in China. I reached out to all three, and each had the same procedure: send them three prototypes, and they in turn will send to me three sample dolls to view the quality of their work.

I was back in touch with Mary Ann to create eight more prototypes, and once complete, I shipped them off to China. Six weeks later I received samples from factory number one, and they were awful. The quality of work was terrible, the fabric was cheap, and the dolls looked downright scary. I was anxious to receive the samples from factory number two, and when I did, the dolls were worse than the first. I was discouraged and not optimistic that factory number three would pull through.

When the package arrived two days later, I was nervous because I didn't know where to turn next. I opened the box, and the dolls were beautiful. Li & Fung, the factory Christy recommended, would produce the Go! Go! Sports Girls. Li & Fung is a supply chain manager, and part of their services include product design and factory sourcing. Their price was a bit higher than the other two, but it was worth the assistance in product design and the high-quality product. To get these sports dolls right, I believed the small details mattered.

When designing the dolls and consulting with Grace, I thought it was important for each doll to have a backpack containing their appropriate sports equipment. Soccer Girl came with a towel and soccer ball, Basketball Girl came with towel and basketball, Golfer Girl came with a towel, golf club, and golf ball.

With Li & Fung's sample dolls in hand I still faced a mountain of obstacles. I needed an attorney to help me with trademarking. I needed liability insurance. I needed to secure domains, build a website and online store, create barcodes, learn about shipping logistics from Hong Kong to Chicago, and abide by ASTM International toy testing standards.

ASTM International is an international standards organization that develops and publishes voluntary consensus technical standards for a wide range of materials, products, systems, and services. These standards are mandatory to sell a product in the United States and requires plush dolls to be tested for heavy metals, lead, physical and mechanical use, and flammability. This does not come at a cheap price, which is factored into the cost of the doll and is very expensive for a small business. In addition, each doll required a warning label that stated the product was not for children under three years old. There was a required size for this label that needed to be sewn into the body of the doll, and it was also required that the warning be printed on the doll's hangtag.

I felt like once I figured out one area, another unknown would surface, costing more money. I realized that creating a doll was not so simple. I was losing confidence, had a lot of fear, and questioned if I could really do this. Making matters worse, people around me questioned the value and potential of my entrepreneurial pursuits.

While on a jog one afternoon, a man I knew from the neighborhood waved, motioning me over. I obliged, and he trotted closer to meet me.

"I've been wanting to ask you a question," he said.

I smiled and said sure. He started by asking how my new business was going—everyone, it seemed, knew what I was up to. After a few formalities he made clear his intention.

"Why do you think girls need to be empowered?"

He went on to explain that his wife, daughters, and the women in his office were already empowered and didn't need any more empowering. He wasn't convinced my product was needed or a good idea.

So many things went through my mind: *Buddy, I am on a run to clear my head and you're ruining the moment. You didn't want to ask me anything; you wanted to tell me your opinion. I really don't care if you are convinced or not. Feel threatened by empowered women, much? Did you really think your "words of wisdom" would make me think, "hum, you're right, my product isn't needed"? Who are you to say the women in your life don't need any more empowering? You're a clueless jerk!*

But I didn't say any of these things. Instead, I calmly pointed out how he is fortunate the women in his life are strong and empowered, but this is not the norm. I went on to explain while great strides have been made toward equality over the years, there's still a lot of work to do and pointed out that research shows when women and girls are empowered, their communities—not just our small community in the western suburbs of Chicago, but communities throughout the world—are more prosperous and stable.

62

"Do you believe your daughters should have equal opportunities?" I asked.

"Of course," he said.

"I'm happy to hear you're a feminist," I said, taking the opportunity to share the definition with him—the political, economic, and social equality of the sexes. I suggested he research feminism and equality and offer his time to help other women feel the same empowerment the women in his life feel.

I saw this over and over throughout the last decade as I championed my girl-empowerment brand. So many men I knew believed in the power of the women they *knew* and could articulate the importance of equality in *general*, but when it came to fighting for women's rights and equality—fighting for half the world's population—they didn't show the same support.

I continued on my run, exasperation fueling my every step.

When I started developing a doll line to empower girls—really empower girls—I honestly didn't anticipate I would need to fight so hard to get a sports-themed doll on store shelves. I was so excited about the possibilities, I glossed over what I knew deep down, and had known for most of my life: our culture is two-faced when it comes to true equality.

PART 2

Disrupting the Pink Aisle
on Behalf of Parents
and Their Daughters

CHAPTER 9

SIDELINED BY STEREOTYPES

"Asking you to give me equal rights implies that they
are yours to give. Instead, I must demand that you
stop trying to deny me the rights all people deserve."
— *Elizabeth Peratrovich*

I graduated from high school in 1982 and attended community college for a semester. After sitting on the sidelines for four-plus years, I was excited to move from my hometown, spread my wings, and attend a large university.

Once at Indiana University in January of 1983, I became more outspoken and took on leadership positions, which paid off my senior year when the administration asked me and another student to be liaisons between IU and singer John Mellencamp, who lived in a neighboring town. Mellencamp had asked the university for years if he could hold a concert at Memorial Stadium, but his request was always denied due to the potential damage to the grass on the field. This year was different. The university was switching from grass to turf and Mellencamp's request was granted. I got to know Mellencamp, had dinner at his house multiple times with his band and wife, and worked with the crew of MTV, who filmed the event. On April 26, 1986, 43,000 people packed Memorial Stadium for one of Mellencamp's greatest shows.

What I learned from that experience—which could never be replicated in a classroom—was an ability to step into a completely unfamiliar process, use my intelligence and common sense to execute a plan, and gain competency, not only for the specific tasks of organizing a large-scale event, but in moving through the world with confidence. As a result of that experience, I am rarely intimidated by people's power and fame, so there is seldom a situation where I don't feel I can't ask questions, advocate for a position, or own my expertise.

Two weeks after that concert, I graduated with a degree in psychology and a minor in business. (I started with communications, then changed to design, knowledge that later served me well as an entrepreneur and product developer.) What I had known since I was a little girl was that I wanted to be an entrepreneur. When I pictured myself as a grown up, I saw myself in charge of my own company. While I didn't have a big business idea to pursue after graduating, I held on to that dream. I figured experience in the working world would not only provide practical experience for running a business but also lead to the next step in that dream.

One week after I graduated, I had my first interview with a company in Chicago. In the interview room a young man my age was interviewing for a position with the company too. We were brought into rooms separately to meet different people for approximately two hours, and at the end we met back in a conference room. The company's human resource employee thanked both of us for our time, and as the young man and I were about to leave, the woman asked me if I would stay for one more test. I immediately felt I had a leg up on this job as I watched the young man walk out of the conference room.

"Sure, what kind of test?" I asked.

"Typing."

My heart sunk. But I wasn't going to slink back into the sidelines.

"Why am I staying to take a typing test but not the guy who just left?"

She looked at me sternly and said, "It's just the way it's done."

I was angry, but I reluctantly took the typing test. I didn't do well, and I didn't care, because there was no way in hell I was going to work for that company.

I believed women were equal to men and assumed the "real world" operated on that belief as well. In the 1980s half of all college graduates were women, and women were earning a steadily rising share of all advanced degrees. Job opportunities were promising. In 1985 women's share of professional jobs was at 49 percent, and their share of management jobs was at 36 percent.[1] As encouraged as I was, the typing incident gave me pause. Women were succeeding to be sure, but at what cost? It was suddenly hard for me to square how women were making such advances when I was pigeonholed into taking a typing test on my first job interview.

Chicago was buzzing with excitement in 1986: the Chicago Bears won Super Bowl XX, and Oprah Winfrey opened Harpo Studios in the Near West Side neighbor-

---

1   George Guilder, "Women in the Work Force" (The Atlantic, September 1, 1986), https://www.theatlantic.com/magazine/archive/1986/09/women-in-the-work-force/304924/.

hood of Chicago. I couldn't wait to move into the city with my college roommate, Roxanne, but couldn't afford to yet. I reluctantly moved back in with my parents. I needed to find a good job that could provide financial independence but didn't require a typing test.

I succeeded in finding a job in the hotel industry working for Sheraton Hotels but failed to take a position that didn't require typing for someone else. I swallowed my pride because I needed the money but continued looking for another job. Every time I sat down to type I felt resentful. Typing represented everything I was working to rise above. Each keystroke pecked away at my confidence.

Fortunately, the next job search only took a few months. I took a sales position with The Ritz-Carlton National Sales office at 444 N Michigan Avenue, one of the coolest locations in Chicago. The position was to represent and sell all Ritz-Carlton Hotels throughout the world to companies in Chicago and the Midwest. It was a new office for Ritz-Carlton, and I was part of the start-up team, which consisted of a group of amazing young women and a few mediocre men...who were our bosses.

I learned quickly what Michelle Obama said so well in a 2018 interview with Oprah when asked how she got over feeling intimidated sitting at big tables filled with smart, powerful men: "You realize pretty quickly that a lot of them aren't that smart." But these men were our bosses, and while they eventually were all fired, Ritz-Carlton never promoted any of the women. They kept hiring mediocre men, and the cycle would repeat.

With my new position came a salary increase, which allowed me financial independence, and, in the summer of 1987, Roxanne and I moved to our first apartment in Lincoln Park.

Summers in Chicago are spectacular, warm with a cool breeze off Lake Michigan. Winters are a different story, cold with gale winds off Lake Michigan. Ritz-Carlton had a strict dress code for women that didn't pair well with Chicago winters: we were required to wear skirts or dresses and nylons but no tights. At first, I didn't think much of it, but by the time winter rolled around I started to become bitter both physically and mentally. Commuting in Chicago requires standing and waiting outside for a bus or the "L," and doing this in a dress or skirt and nylons in the cold, wind, and snow is crazy, not to mention dangerous.

I wanted to keep my job, but I wanted to change the ancient dress code, which also included no earrings larger than a quarter, and no red or bright colored fingernail polish—neutral shades only. My female co-workers and I made our arguments about this ridiculous requirement to the corporate office, and after a few years they finally allowed women to wear pants, but they were very specific that it had to be a "pantsuit." It couldn't be nice pants and a blazer but a matching pantsuit. They went so far as to send an HR representative from Atlanta to give a fashion show with allowable pantsuit ensembles. This victory in the corporate world made up for my near drowning experience in the typing pool.

During this time, I met a guy who wasn't like the men I was working with. He was funny, smart, and a law student at the University of Chicago. I also found him (and still do) super cute. He was witty and clever, and I had never been around another person who made me laugh as hard as Steve. Even during disagreements, he always found a way to make me laugh and smile. He showed me the power of laughter, which has helped us through tough times throughout our entire marriage.

Steve and I married in 1989 and moved to Hyde Park, a neighborhood on the south side of Chicago and home to University of Chicago, so he could finish his final year. I worked long hours at Ritz-Carlton, and he studied and did most of the housework and cooking. Steve grew up in a home with progressive parents, so when it came to managing our home, we divided and conquered without preconceived ideas about who should do what based on gender roles.

After graduation, Steve took a position at a large city law firm, and we moved back to Lincoln Park. I was growing tired of the Ritz and management's support of the "Peter Principle," the continuous promotion of men who were given the opportunity to rise to their level of incompetence while competent and high-achieving women were continuously overlooked.

When I became an entrepreneur in 1991, I believed I could insulate myself from sexism in the workplace, and for a time with my gift basket business, I did. Ironically, starting the Go! Go! Sports Girls, a brand that defied gender stereotypes, put me back into a position where I had to fight against them more intensely.

CHAPTER 10

BIG BREAK AT THE US OPEN

"The simple things are also the most extraordinary
things, and only the wise can see them."
– *Paulo Coelho*

When it comes to "things" or "stuff," I'm a minimalist.
(Except for shoes. I really love shoes!) Overall, I
don't keep much, and I don't like clutter. I wouldn't call
myself a neat freak; I just don't like unnecessary stuff
everywhere. When my firstborn, Peter, came home from
college for the first time, he paused as he entered his bed-
room, which I had cleaned, organized, and decluttered.
He said sarcastically, "Well, Mom, thanks for getting rid
of my entire childhood."

For some reason, I kept most of my paperwork, note
pads, scratch pads, and first marketing plan of the Go!
Go! Sports Girls that I created in 2007. For the most part,
the goals I set, big and small, I achieved. My Purpose of
Product, which I adhered to for more than a decade, read:

Go! Go! Sports Girls are soft, plush, sports-themed
dolls designed to encourage physical activity among youths
three to twelve years, regardless of race or socioeconomic
class. Along with supporting materials, the dolls' whole-
some, positive images will promote self-appreciation and

the benefits of daily exercise, healthy eating and sleeping habits, self-esteem, and overall healthy life-skills.

Go! Go! Sports Girls are age and size appropriate. They do not encourage an older or overly mature image. The image is innocent with a subtle yet strong message: appreciate and be true to yourself!

I included a mission statement, product attributes, pricing, distribution, timeframe, target market, competitive analysis, website, sales goals, and more. Reading through it again more than a decade later, everything still resonates; it was well thought out from the start. I was determined to encourage all children to Dream Big and Go For It!

While I was on the right track in the spring of 2008, I continued to look for the right partners. One of my goals was to find a good marketing company that could build and manage my website, create marketing material, a logo, and provide expert advice. I reached out to friends again asking for recommendations and received a few in Chicago and New York. I spoke with them all, and while they were all great, they were too expensive.

I was desperate to find this big and affordable puzzle piece when a friend mentioned a start-up marketing company by a sharp young man named Keith Booton. Keith and I met, and I immediately liked him. Keith was the perfect person for the job, and his new company, Boost Marketing, became my amazing, kind, creative and affordable marketing team. It was a time when I referred to what Ina had taught me, and I trusted my instincts.

Over the years, Keith has grown an impressive marketing firm, which is now called Ivor Andrew. I'm not surprised by his success. He went above and beyond my expectations, creating videos, designing and creating my tradeshow material and space; he became a business counselor and trusted friend. He encouraged me to step over my fear and move forward, which ultimately lead to my first sale.

On a warm spring afternoon—the kind of day in the Midwest where everyone ventures out of hibernation, and every living species feels alive and happy—I was feeling strong and capable after getting in a workout when I had a thought. What if I called the United States Tennis Association (USTA) to see if they would buy Tennis Girl Gracie for the US Open in August? I had no connection with them; I had just been a big tennis fan my whole life.

Then doubt set in. I didn't want to embarrass myself. What if they said no? As an entrepreneur I have learned "what if" thoughts are common and can hold you back. I decided to step over my "what if" fear and flip it. "What if" I give them a call, and they like my product? I knew I needed to be quick before another negative "what if" popped into my head. From my car in a bagel shop parking lot, I looked up the number and dialed. A receptionist answered, and I asked to be transferred to the person in charge of purchasing for the US Open. It worked, and I was quickly connected to their merchandising manager, Jennifer.

Jennifer was friendly and asked me to quickly give her a description of what I had to offer. Excited and nervous, I had to calmly pull it together and give her my best pitch. Within five minutes, she responded, "I love what you are doing. I'll take 500." You can only imagine my excitement. My first order was for 500 dolls!

I soon received my first purchase order from the USTA for sale at the 2008 US Open. There was only one problem: they required a June delivery date. By boat, my product wouldn't arrive until September. My only option was to air freight the 500 dolls directly to New York. That meant I wouldn't make any money on the dolls. I believed it was worth the PR.

On June 10, 2008, I placed another order with Li & Fung for the first nine Go! Go! Sports Girls: Tennis Girl Gracie, Soccer Girl Cassie, Runner Girl Ella, Basketball Girl Taye, Golfer Girl Brooke, Gymnastics Girl Maya, Swimmer Girl Suzi, Softball Girl Sam, and Dancer Girl M.C. for a total of 5,035 dolls that I imagined would be the talk of toy buyers everywhere.

I am often asked the question, "When looking back, is there one thing you regret or could change?" My answer is always, yes. I wish I had started with fewer styles. Not nine but perhaps four to test the waters with a smaller investment and risk. I also would have started local. I live in a big city, and it would have been a better test market than going big and launching at Toy Fair in New York City. Could have, should have, would have. Overall, I don't have many regrets. And at the time, with the momentum from my US Open order, I couldn't fathom failure.

In August of 2008, Go! Go! Sports Girl, Tennis Girl Gracie debuted at the US Open, and all 500 dolls sold out in six days. I attended the US Open that year, which is held at the Billie Jean King National Tennis Center in Flushing Meadows, NY, with four of my closest tennis-loving friends. It was exciting to see little girls carrying Tennis Girl Gracie throughout the park, the dolls displayed at the kiosks, and seeing the doll on the jumbotron in the Arthur Ashe Stadium, the US Open's main stadium.

At one point, my excitement got the best of me as I saw a sweet young girl around seven years old carrying Tennis Girl Gracie in one hand, swinging as she walked, the other holding the hand of her mother. I smiled as she walked toward me and my friends. I bent down in front of her, looked her in the eyes, and asked excitedly, "Do you like your dolly?" She and her parents looked at me with a somewhat mortified look and said nothing as they politely smiled and continued walking past me. My friends quickly said, "Yeah, you've got to stop doing that! They don't know you designed the doll. They think you're some creepy lady." I understood, but it was still hard to contain my joy and excitement.

In many of my keynote presentations, I speak about the small moments in life that can have a big impact. I encourage audiences to recognize those moments and not dismiss them. As an example, I point out three important small moments in my entrepreneurial journey that had a big impact and took my business to the next level. The first of those three small moments turned into my first sale to the USTA.

With the success at the US Open, I was confident I had a good test, a good product, and a good message. My next goal was to launch the line of nine dolls at the New York Toy Fair in February of 2009. I believed the Go! Go! Sports Girls would take Toy Fair by storm. I had the next big thing, and everyone would agree that it's important to give girl's strong, smart, and powerful images. The Go! Go! Sports Girls were the beginning of the solution — at least that's what I thought.

There was yet another obstacle to face, and this one didn't have anything to do with gender stereotypes or girl empowerment. In September 2008, the great recession hit. It was a terrible time to launch a new product, but everything was in place, and there was no turning back.

CHAPTER 11

GO! GO! SPORTS GIRLS VERSUS FASHION DOLLS

"If she can see it, she can be it."
— Geena Davis

The morning of Saturday, February 14, 2009, Valentine's Day, I kissed Steve and the kid's good-bye, all of them hugging me and wishing me good luck, and drove to the airport to catch a flight to New York City to attend my first North American International Toy Fair. I was excited, nervous, and scared. A lot of "what ifs" were popping into my head, but my excitement pushed them aside. My cousin Toni offered to help me and flew in from Washington DC to meet me in NYC. Toy Fair is a four-day trade show, and she was the perfect, outgoing, fun, and energetic person to spend time with and help launch and sell the Go! Go! Sports Girls.

Weeks prior, I shipped 200 dolls, the backdrop for my booth that Keith had designed, a table and chairs, display stands, and two five-foot Go! Go! Sports Girls—Soccer Girl Cassie and Tennis Girl Gracie dolls—that Li & Fung created to help me stand out at the show. After meeting Toni at LaGuardia Airport, we went directly to the Javits

Center to begin the set up and decorate my small exhibit booth #2078.

Unable to sleep, Toni and I woke up early the next morning with excitement and anticipation to sell, sell, sell. Wanting to look sporty to sell sports dolls, Toni and I dressed in matching Go! Go! Sports Girls uniforms: pink polos with the Go! Go! Sports Girls logo, khaki pants, and gym shoes. Exiting our hotel, the morning air was crisp, and we began our seven-block walk, coffee in hand, to the largest toy trade show in the western hemisphere.

At 10:00 a.m. on Sunday, February 15, with more than 1,000 exhibitors ready to showcase more than 150,000 toy and entertainment products, the doors opened to a crowd of retailers, buyers, and press. Toni and I were confident in my product and mission and eager to meet with buyers, but my booth was toward the back of the building, so it took a long fifteen minutes before we started to see people. Buyers from small and large retail stores came to meet with us. Sears showed a lot of interest, as did a sporting goods store from Denmark, but by the end of the day we had zero orders. I wasn't worried because I was told this was how it worked, and orders would be placed the following days. With the first day behind us, exhausted, and our backs and feet aching, Toni and I left the Javits Center, determined to find a great restaurant and a glass of wine.

On Monday—day two of Toy Fair—the doors opened an hour earlier at 9:00 a.m., and the crowd of retailers, buyers, and press streamed in the convention center. It felt a bit like Groundhog Day; same place, same outfit, same spiel, but with our minds, backs, and feet rested, we were feeling energetic, optimistic, and ready for orders. By the end of the day, I had ten orders. They were small orders for about twenty-four to fifty dolls each, but they were orders, and I was thrilled.

I also had a lot of press come to my booth wanting to write about the Go! Go! Sports Girls. The US market size for the total toy industry is approximately $27 billion, so it's big business, and reporters and bloggers are looking for the next cool toy and trend. There are journalists filming, taking photographs, and interviewing many exhibitors, so when they came to my booth, I was excited and reinforced my message: Girls play sports, and so should their dolls.

With day two behind us, Toni and I set out to find another great restaurant and another glass of wine, the best part of Groundhog Day.

As Toni and I entered the Javits Center on day three, we felt a different vibe and buzz in the air. Exhibitors were discussing the trade show's low attendance and the few orders they had received. Since it was my first Toy Fair, I had nothing to compare to, but the exhibitors were feeling the effects of the recession.

Day three brought more press to my booth as well as buyers coming back for the second or third time, contemplating on whether to buy the Go! Go! Sports Girls. Toni and I tried our best to convince buyers that girls like more than fashion, and they should buy the dolls. We rattled off my researched statistics: seventeen million girls in the US play a sport; sports and physical activity are associated with greater self-esteem and positive body image, and so on. We explained all with conviction yet little success. One by one the buyers declined, and every rejection response contained the word "fashion."

"I love your product. My daughter plays soccer, and she would love Soccer Girl, but I can't buy the Go! Go! Sports Girls because ultimately girls like fashion."

"Your product isn't mainstream. It isn't a fashion doll. When it becomes mainstream, can you give me a call?"

"For some reason girls always gravitate toward fashion dolls."

"Great idea, but girls like fashion. Can you create a fashion doll?"

Exhausted and tired of being polite, my response to creating a fashion doll was, "That's my point! As a mother of a daughter and as a woman, I am positive that girls like more than fashion. They have other interests, and it's time to represent who they are right now—strong, smart, and brave."

I want to be clear that I have nothing against fashion. In fact, I find fashion beautiful, interesting, colorful, and I have a strong appreciation for exhibiting one's personal style. However, I'd like to argue that girls gravitate toward fashion dolls because there are seventy-five brands of fashion dolls marketed to girls with few other options. How can a girl gravitate to something that isn't offered? It's like a grocer saying their customers gravitate toward peanut butter when their shelves are stocked with seventy-five brands of peanut butter. What would happen if they introduce almond, cashew, hazelnut, and pistachio butters? I'd bet the peanut butter revenue doesn't decrease, and the overall nut butter revenue booms.

Overall, my experience at Toy Fair was positive. I received orders, and the press was drawn to my product and story, but I started to see the battle looming in my future: those who believed profits were tied to tired stereotypes versus banking on representing a bold new idea for girls. Mainstream ideas never create change, and I was creating change. I dug in my heels.

CHAPTER 12

WHAT PARENTS WANT FOR THEIR DAUGHTERS

"It took me quite a long time to develop a voice, and now that I have it, I am not going to be silent."
— Madeleine Albright

Generally, I am pretty even keeled, but this business tested my patience by taking me on many highs and many lows. Getting to Toy Fair in February 2009, was certainly a high, but returning I had never felt so low. The overriding message I heard from buyers was to take my unique product and turn it into something familiar. There was no way I was going to create a fashion doll. There were approximately seventy-five fashion doll brands on the market and zero sports dolls. I was answering the unquestioned assumption, and I was filling a much-needed void in the marketplace.

The very reason I created this doll was to give girls something different, but what the doll buyers were asking for signaled to me I wasn't really in the doll or toy business. If I were, I would have listened to what the buyers wanted and changed my focus to meet their demand. My lack of conformity signaled to me I wasn't in it to lead a successful toy brand; I was in it to change the industry. I was on a mission to give girls better choices and the respect they deserve.

Determined to get my message and product out to the world, I wasn't exactly sure how. The thought was overwhelming because I realized my biggest competitor was Barbie with her parent company, Mattel. I never expected this, but I quickly learned Mattel is the biggest competitor of every company in the toy industry. How could I compete with them? How could I set myself apart from them and the other seventy-five doll brands? I didn't have the resources, knowledge, talent, budget, or a large team to compete. But I knew I had one thing no one else had, and I had a feeling it could work. I had a story, and the media at Toy Fair showed interest.

One of the perks of being an exhibitor at Toy Fair is that the Toy Association shares the list of media outlets who attended the show, including email addresses of journalists. I decided to do a PR blitz and contact everyone on the list and tell them my story. I Googled "how to write a media pitch," and I began sending individual emails, making each one personal when possible. In the back of my mind, I kept thinking about the dolls selling out at the US Open. I felt sure if people knew about them, they would buy them. My PR blitz was my way to get the word out and advertise without spending money.

I was having success and heard back from bloggers and did many interviews. I sent follow up emails to individuals I hadn't heard back from and then another and another. I persisted. Then a few months later I received an email that read:

Hi Jodi!

My name is Alice and I'm an editor at *Shape* magazine. You recently sent our editor in chief an email and she just loved the idea behind the Go! Go! Sports Girls. We'd like to feature the dolls and you as a "Woman who inspires us" in our November issue. Is there a time early next week we could talk on the phone? I'd like to know where the idea came from and how you turned it into a reality. Also, could you email me a photo of yourself and also one of the dolls?

Thanks!
Alice

This was big. *Shape* magazine wanted to do a feature on me, and not just any feature, but a "Woman who inspires us" feature. This was definitely one of my highs, and I felt this interview was not only about my product but also about the empowering message I was sending to women and girls that they are the leaders we need to make a change in our world.

In addition to my PR blitz, I decided to send the nine Go! Go! Sports Girls dolls to the Oppenheim Toy Portfolio for review. The Oppenheim Toy Portfolio is one of the top awards in the toy industry and is highly respected. It was started by Joanne and Stephanie Oppenheim, a mother-daughter team, and only outstanding products are selected by their testers and are awarded one of four honors:

Platinum Award: These represent the most innovative, engaging new products of the year.

Gold Seal Award: Given to outstanding new products that enhance the lives of children.

Blue Chip Classic Award: Reserved for classic products that should not be missed just because they weren't invented yesterday.

SNAP Award: Our Special Needs Adaptable Product Award is given to products that can be used by or easily adapted for children with special needs.[1]

I didn't think I had much of a chance, but sometimes it's good to swing for the fences. I had nothing to lose. I didn't hear from them after my submission for a few months, so I thought the Go! Go! Sports Girls weren't selected. I tried not to feel disappointment but couldn't help wondering why. Then in September of 2009 I received in the mail an eight-by-ten inch envelope from Oppenheim Toy Portfolio. I carefully opened it not knowing what to expect, and in it was a letter and certificate congratulating me on receiving not one but two Oppenheim awards: the Gold Seal Award and Platinum Award, their highest award. The letter also stated that the Go! Go! Sports Girls had been selected to be featured on Stephanie's *Today Show* segment, "This year, buy toys with lasting playing value," in December.

Another high point! I was ecstatic and immediately emailed Joanne and Stephanie to thank them. Over the

---

1   Oppenheim Toy Portfolio, https://www.toyportfolio.com/ .

years, Joanne and Stephanie have been great support-ers of my mission and product, and I am honored to know them.

There was a good spike in sales in December of 2009, and with all the great press and awards, I was sure a large retailer would pick up my line in 2010.

CHAPTER 13

WOMEN SUPPORTING WOMEN

"One woman can make a difference,
but together we can rock the world."
– Merle Shain

On becoming my own public relations person, I learned that a relationship with the media can result in all kinds of outcomes — not just a mention in a news article or magazine profile. Of course, publicity can be good for sales, but publicity also brought forth new opportunities I hadn't considered before.

Hi Jodi,

I just discovered your dolls today. As an active mom of three active girls I am thrilled. I may sell you out of Ella.... As a writer and blogger I can't wait to spread the word.

As I read about each doll, an idea clicked. Aside from personally wanting a triathlon doll (hint hint) I have written a children's book about a little girl who finishes her first triathlon, called "I'm a Triathlete!" That character embodies the same spirit as your dolls. I thought it would be wonderful to partner with you to make my character come alive in the form of a doll—the book and doll could be sold together. I'm dreaming big.... I would love to talk.

Sincerely,
Kara

Kara Douglass Thom emailed me on November 19, 2009. She read about my dolls from another fitness blogger, who learned about the dolls from the *Shape* magazine article. I loved that she was sporty, had three little girls, and was dreaming big, and I immediately knew I would like her. I wanted to talk to her and learn more about her idea. I emailed her back to schedule a time to speak the following week, and I was right—I really liked her. She was down to earth, funny, passionate, and enthusiastic about writing a book for the Go! Go! Sports Girls.

Kara lived in the Minneapolis area, and in addition to three little girls who were between ages four and six, she had a little boy, born earlier that year. We spoke for a good hour, and she told me about her triathlon book for adults, *Becoming an Ironman: First Encounters with the Ultimate Endurance Event*, her children's book, *See Mom Run*, and the book she was in the process of co-authoring (that was published in 2011), *Hot (Sweaty) Mamas: Five Secrets to Life as a Fit Mom*, which I couldn't wait to read. She explained her idea for a Go! Go! Sports Girls book and suggested incorporating fun facts about each sport in each book. I loved the idea of elevating the mission of Go! Go! Sports Girls not only through creative play but also through a story for each doll.

While sports have dominated the subject matter for books marketed to boys, there are few sports series that feature a female protagonist. Girls play sports and so should female characters in books. Not only do girls need to see themselves on the pages they read, but also boys benefit when they open books that mirror today's reality on the playing field.

Kara was on to something, and we were both excited about the possibility of bringing the dolls to life through books, but then a wave of reality hit me. I couldn't afford to pay Kara upfront, and I told her, feeling like I just took a pin to our big, beautiful balloon. Pop! To my surprise, Kara's enthusiasm continued, and she responded, "It's okay. I just really want to be a part of this project." How could I turn down that deal! She was just as passionate as me about girls rising to their full potential and giving them options beyond stereotypes that don't pigeonhole them into thinking they need to be a princess. We agreed that the first book she would write would be for Soccer Girl Cassie. Go! Go! Writer Girl Kara!

Kara blogged about the Go! Go! Sports Girls recanting the reactions of her daughters as they played:

These dolls come dressed for their sport and each have a mini backpack to carry their gear (huge hit!) My daughters started playing immediately and as soon as their Go! Go! Sports Girls had played their own sport they started cross training, which is to say my daughters undressed their dolls and swapped outfits.

"Can my girl run, mama?"

"Of course, she can!" I coaxed. "Tennis players need to run, too."

"My girl can go swimming?"

"I like to run and swim," I tell her. "You like to run and swim, why not?"

The creative sports play continued into the night. There were Go! Go! Sports Girls dreams because the dolls slept with my daughters and in the morning, they were back at it: Swimming, running, playing tennis.

What's interesting to me is that they have many times used sports in their creative play—emulating mom and dad by exercising or in pretend races. However, they've never engaged their dolls in sports play until now. But none of their other dolls have come with running shoes, or swim goggles, or a tennis racquet. Come on! How CUTE is THAT?

The real magic is the positive message these dolls provide to little girls. Fitness is a family value in our house and when I can find toys that support that value, I'm one happy parent.

"The positive message these dolls provide to little girls" are key words that would be used by bloggers and journalists to describe the Go! Go! Sports Girls for the next decade. In addition to *Shape* magazine and *The Today*

Show, the dolls were featured in *Self* and *Parenting* magazines. While my initial reaction from toy buyers was cool at best, the reaction from media and parents was scalding hot. I knew I had a pulse on what our culture wanted. I knew I had a vibe that parents wanted more for their girls too.

CHAPTER 14

HOW MASS MARKETS FAIL GIRLS

"The elevator to success is out of order.
You'll have to use the stairs, one step at a time."
– Joe Girard

When February 2010 arrived, Toni and I were back at Toy Fair. This time I needed a third person to help me and brought another cousin, Tonia. I came armed with great press, reviews, and awards (adding *Creative Child Magazine* Seal of Excellence Award to the list); a possible new children's book; and I had secured the support of Girls on the Run, Girls Inc., and the Women's Sports Foundation. I was sure to grab the attention of a large retailer.

Again, the media was drawn to my story, message, and product, but the buyers were hesitant. One buyer told me he didn't know where he would put the Go! Go! Sports Girls because they didn't fit in the "fashion," "baby," or "sports equipment" categories, so he gave up. I had another buyer tell me my brand was going to be huge one day but didn't want to be the first large retailer to carry it. Another buyer gave me a big compliment, telling me my product was brilliant, but he wasn't confident the dolls would sell because they weren't fashion dolls, so he didn't place an order. And of course, again and again, I heard the "girls like fashion" excuse.

As hard as rejection can be, I knew it really didn't matter how many buyers said no. I only needed one yes.

On the fourth and final day of the show, Jason, a representative from Three Sixty Sales, a manufacturers rep group in Minneapolis entered my booth. He explained he had reviewed my company and thought my product and message were great. He complimented me on accomplishing so much in a short period of time. One of their retail partners was Target. He thought the Go! Go! Sports Girls would be a perfect fit for their stores and asked if he could present the line to the Target girl toy buyer. Heck yeah! It would be another five years and many parents calling for the desegregation of children's products before Target stopped gendering toy aisles in their stores.

I left Toy Fair 2010 feeling similar to how I left Toy Fair 2009, with a few orders, but a lot of interest from the press. Only this time I had an opportunity to meet with Target. That nudge forward was finally happening. People—people with buying power—were starting to take notice of the Go! Go! Sports Girls. Jason called me shortly after Toy Fair and said the Target buyer was interested in meeting on May 26. I would have thirty minutes to present my product.

I hung up the phone, jumped up and down, gave out a little scream of excitement, hugged our dog (an adorable but hyper Portuguese Water Dog we named Scout after one of my favorite characters in one of my favorite books,

To Kill a Mockingbird), then I called Steve to tell him the good news. That was the break I was waiting for.

For the next few months, I studied and researched Target customers: average age, education level, how many kids the average shopper had and their ages, average household income, and sex. I studied their stores to see how and where products were placed and displayed, and I couldn't help fantasizing where the Go! Go! Sports Girls would sit. Their girl toy aisles were a sea of pink, so I believed the Go! Go! Sports Girls would be a welcome non-pink item on store shelves. I prepared a sales deck outlining my research to present to the Target girl toy buyer Darek and his team to convince him what I believed: Target shoppers were the perfect market for the Go! Go! Sports Girls.

The morning of May 26, I flew to Minneapolis. First stop was the Three Sixty Sales office to meet Jason and go over our game plan. That afternoon Jason and I drove a few miles to the Target Headquarters to meet with Darek and his team. The Target Headquarters is impressive and has a very youthful feel, looking more like a college campus than a corporate headquarters. Jason and I got situated in a private conference room, setting up the dolls for display and putting a sales deck at each seat. Shortly after, Darek and his team of four arrived.

I began giving my best presentation, but I quickly felt intimidated. Darek never looked me in the eyes. He studied the dolls as I spoke, carefully picking one up at a time, turning it over then moving to the next doll. I couldn't get a read on how he was feeling or what he was thinking. I wondered, is he listening? I glanced over at Jason who gave me a nod that told me it's okay, keep going, you're doing a good job. I finished, and there was a long, awkward pause. It was Darek's turn to comment, and he wasn't saying anything. He kept turning the dolls over in his hands, examining them closely. I was nervous, and I wasn't confident his response was going to be what I wanted to hear.

Ending the silence, Darek finally looked at me. With a slight smile he said, "You would be a terrible person not to love these dolls. I love them."

He turned to his team, instructed them to get me setup in their system as a vendor and walked out the door. They asked me a few questions and told me what they needed from me. Then the meeting was over.

I was cautiously excited but also in a bit of shock. Everything happened so quickly. As Jason and I left the room I asked him, "What just happened?" He answered, "The best response possible."

Kara knew about my meeting with Target, and our plan was for her to pick me up at Target's headquarters after the meeting. We were excited to finally meet each other in person. Outside the building, Jason congratulated me, we hugged good-bye, and I jumped into Kara's car. I told her the entire story as she drove to a wine bar nearby.

Late that afternoon, I flew back to Chicago and drove directly to a Memorial Day party with friends to celebrate. I believed I had finally hit that moment that would define my big break. The Go! Go! Sports Girls would go on to become an iconic brand and household name, beloved by parents and little girls everywhere. The doll industry would finally be disrupted, and girls would have something to play with that represented their lives as they really lived them. After being hard at work on my idea for nearly two years, I believed I had paid my dues and worked through the process and all the right channels. This was it!

I was optimistic about the future and sometimes I wish I could go back to myself then and break the news to her—that it is better to be cautiously optimistic. I would tell her to hope for the best and plan for the worst.

Instead, with my unburdened optimism I worked with Darek's team the next few weeks to set up Dream Big Toy Company and the Go! Go! Sports Girls as a Target vendor. I emailed Timothy at Li & Fung and told him to be prepared for an order from me in the near future and gave him the amount Target was estimating for their first order—58,000 Go! Go! Sports Girls!

Then the activity went quiet. A few weeks passed, and I waited patiently for the purchase order from Darek. I sent Darek an email asking if he needed additional information from me, telling him I was set to go and asked when I should expect to receive the purchase order. There was no response. I started to worry. A few days went by before I composed a follow up email. Immediately after hitting the send button, the phone rang. I checked the number and saw it was Darek. My stomach immediately went into knots.

Darek's voice was low and uncheerful. He skipped pleasantries and began to explain that he and his team had a meeting with his boss about the Go! Go! Sports Girls, and she didn't feel they were a good fit for Target stores.

She felt they were too similar to another brand of plush dolls they carried in their stores a few years before that didn't sell well. He broke the news that they would not be moving forward with the brand.

Not willing to take the rejection so easily, I asked if the other brand they had carried were sports dolls? He answered that they were not sports dolls but fashion dolls. I tried to make my case that the two doll brands weren't similar at all, but he quickly cut me off with an apology and again said they were not moving forward.

My big break shattered into a tiny thousand pieces.

I sat at my desk in shock. I felt numb and knew the pain, sadness, and disappointment would slowly creep into every part of my body, and it did. For days I felt depressed and defeated. I tried not to think about my business, but I couldn't stop the negative thoughts, especially thoughts of giving up. I thought of the naysayers, and maybe they were right with their negative comments. So, I cleaned. I cleaned the entire house for days because I'm a nervous cleaner. Some psychologists say that cleaning gives people a sense of mastery and control over their environment. I fit into this description perfectly.

My sparkling clean house did not lift my spirits nor give me a sense of control. I laid in my bed early one morning awake mulling over the Target debacle when I had a rare but welcomed optimistic thought: I started this business less than two years ago, and I got far with Target. I grabbed the attention of Target and their buyers. They don't give this type of attention to every product, only good products, products that have potential. Girls deserve more, my daughter deserves more, women deserve more. Jumping out of bed, I knew I had to persist.

From that moment on, I put my mission ahead of any disappointment and sadness I experienced. To this day I think about my Target moment and how that helped me grow emotionally.

CHAPTER 15

SEARCHING FOR FEMALE CHARACTERS IN CHILDREN'S BOOKS

"To all the little girls watching…never doubt that you are valuable and powerful and deserving of every chance and opportunity in the world."
– Hillary Clinton

When my children were little, there were a handful of brands they loved: Winnie the Pooh, Arthur, Clifford the Big Red Dog, Caillou, and Barney. They loved the books, television shows, and owned and played with many of the plush characters. These are positive and healthy brands, but they have one thing in common: they all center around a male main character.

Kara noticed this too. Why are there so few girls in children's television shows and books? Whether they are human, animal, train, or truck, the main characters are almost always male. Knowing girls deserve to see and read about big dreams by strong, smart, and brave women and boys deserve to see and read these stories too, Kara and I wanted to be the change. First, we needed a better understanding of this lack of female characters and set out to study the problem. After extensive research and reading over the years, we realized we weren't the only ones aware of this disproportionate representation in children's books.

A 2011 Florida State University study of 6,000 children's books published from 1900 to 2000 found that "no more than 33 percent of children's books published in any given year contain central characters that are adult women or female animals, but adult men and male animals appear in up to 100 percent of books."[1]

According to *Good Night Stories for Rebel Girls* authors Francesca Cavallo and Elena Favilli's eye-opening video, 'The Ugly Truth of Children's Books," in more than 5,000 children's books, 25 percent had zero female characters, and less than 20 percent showed women with a job, compared to more than 80 percent of male characters[2].

In a study by Geena Davis Institute on Gender in Media, examining gender and race representation in the top one hundred grossing family films in 2017, "Male leads continue to outnumber female leads two-to-one, and protagonists of color rarely appear as leads. When it comes to screen time and speaking time, female characters receive far less face time and speak less often than male characters."[3] However, their findings found that female-

---

1   Janice McCabe, "From Peter Rabbit to Curious George, FSU Study Finds 100 Years of Gender Bias in Children's Books" (Florida State University News, October 21, 2016).

2   *The Ugly Truth of Children's Books (Rebel Girls, 2017).*

3   *Gender and Race Representations in the Top Family Films of 2017 (n.d.), https://geenadavisinstitute.org/wp-content/uploads/2024/01/see-jane-100-report-2017.pdf.*

led family films grossed 38.1 percent more on average than male-led films.

When I was young, I was never fond of fairytales. I found them frightening because in many of the stories, the loving mother dies and is replaced by a cruel stepmother. I always hoped the lead female characters would take control of her circumstances and find courage and strength to somehow become a cool badass woman and save the day. To my disappointment, that never happened. Instead, she was always rescued by some guy who was usually a prince. I understand fairytales can inspire imagination, but they are riddled with damaging stereotypes.

According to the Let Toys Be Toys campaign, "Just like labeling toys 'for girls' or 'for boys', books send out very limiting messages to children about what kinds of things are appropriate for girls or for boys. Blue covers, with themes of action and adventure, robots, space, trucks and pirates contrast with a riot of pink sparkles, fairies, princesses, flowers and butterflies. But real children's interests are a lot more diverse, and more interesting, than that." [4]

Shelly Boyum-Breen began writing and publishing the Shelly Bean the Sports Queen series in 2006 after flipping through a Scholastic order form and seeing nothing but books on cheerleading and horseback riding targeted toward girls. At the time, she was working in sales for the WNBA's Lynx and had started a nonprofit to help girls be able to afford to play sports. She knew from experience more girls than ever were playing sports. She was

---

4   Let toys be toys: Home (n.d.), http://LetToysBeToys.org.uk.

her high school's star basketball player, went on to play basketball and tennis in college and then to coach at the high school and college level.[5]

When she was younger, she could never see herself in books, so she never enjoyed reading. "I was not a princess. I was not a girl on the prairie. I was not a boy. My passion and life revolved around playing sports. There wasn't anything that connected me to that and there were no sports books for girls."

Prior to writing her first book, she discovered that less than 2 percent of children's books that are published every year have a female character who is physically active in the book. And this includes riding on a magic carpet with a boy! When pitching publishers and literary agents, she thought, "I'm handing them their golden ticket, the next J.K. Rowling. New York is going to be calling. I'm going to be on *Good Morning America* with Robin Roberts in no time!" Little did she know, over the next three years she would be a collector of rejection letters. She has never given up and has talked to over 100,000 kids throughout the US and has sold over 15,000 books.

Another problem is the myth that books about girls aren't suitable for boys. Children's literature blogger Betsy Bird states, "There is an unspoken understanding in children's books that a boy won't read about a girl, which I think is a self-fulfilling prophecy." I agree. Thinking that a boy won't read about a girl is not only foolish but antiquated. Boyum-Breen found that over half the readers of

5   Jeremy Millsop, "Athletics: Shooting Hoops with Shelly Boyum-Breen" (Brainerd Dispatch, March 12, 2019), https://www.brainerddispatch.com/sports/athletics-shooting-hoops-with-shelly-boyum-breen.

the Shelly Bean books are boys. A book that has a female lead character does not mean it's a book for girls.

At the age of five, my youngest son's favorite book series was Amelia Bedelia by Peggy Parish. I will never forget his laughter and enjoyment as Amelia Bedelia performed comical and incorrect actions from taking words too literally. I will admit I begged him some nights to choose another book other than Amelia Bedelia because her repetitive misunderstandings were driving me crazy, but he was hooked, and he loved this book series with a female protagonist.

With the Go! Go! Sports Girls book series, Kara and I were going to give children female lead characters who played sports. We were going to provide a much-needed choice in the book marketplace, one that was age-appropriate, represented the way girls really lived, and emphasized what a girl's body could do rather than what it looked like.

In March of 2010, Kara wrote Soccer Girl Cassie's Story. Cassie, the female lead character, was strong, smart, kind, and brave, and I loved the sprinkle of soccer facts throughout the book. It was positive and smart. It had nothing to do with mean girls, princess, or boy problems, typical narratives in books marketed to girls. It was an engaging story about a friendly rivalry that taught kids the meaning of teamwork.

She was already hard at work writing Swimmer Girl Suzy's Story and had the framework for Runner Girl Ella's Story. Her inspiration came from watching her own daughters experiment with the very sports she was writing about.

But after the Target experience, I struggled with how to move forward with Kara's book. I felt without a significant order in hand, my line didn't warrant the addition of a new product, nor could I afford it. I discussed this with Kara, who continued to write anyway despite not having a clear plan to move forward. She was as determined as me to create change and make the Go! Go! Sports Girls brand a success. She became my writer, my consultant, my trustworthy, kind, and dear friend.

With Kara as my teammate, my changemaker ambitions grew. I was not only going to create change in the toy industry, but now *we* were going to create change in the publishing industry. The same gender stereotyping battle I was fighting with the toys would now include books.

CHAPTER 16

DISCONNECT BETWEEN TOY AWARDS AND SALES

"We cannot all succeed when half of us are held
back. We call upon our sisters around the world
to be brave—to embrace the strength within
themselves and realize their full potential."
— Malala Yousafzai

2010 and 2011 brought more press and more awards
but barely enough orders to keep me afloat. I still
wasn't taking a salary and put every penny back into
the business.

On the heels of the Oppenheim Toy Portfolio Awards,
in 2010 I received Dr. Toy's 10 Best Socially Responsible
Toys Award and their prestigious 10 Best Toys of the Year
Award. I now had two of the top awards in the toy industry. I was sure this industry-led credibility would bring
more respect from toy buyers.

The awards gave me further reason to connect with
the media. I did more than a hundred interviews with
bloggers, newspapers, magazines, and television shows. I
had a story, and I was right: it resonated with people. The
Chicago Tribune did a feature on me titled "Remarkable
Person," I was interviewed on *Windy City Live*, a Chicago

morning show, and my favorite press came from *Good Housekeeping* who named the Go! Go! Sports Girls as one of the "12 Top Trends from Toy Fair 2011."

With each published interview came emails from women all over the country: *"Thank you for fighting for our daughters and girls and thank you for providing a much-needed positive imaged doll. I wish the Go! Go! Sports Girls were around when I was younger."* I loved all the press and feedback I was receiving, but I noticed the disparity. Why was I getting so much positive feedback but few orders from toy buyers?

There was one more top toy award I hadn't received— the Toy of the Year (TOTY) Award sponsored by the Toy Association. The award criteria included creativity and originality, design and quality, play value, marketing and promotion, and sales and marketplace acceptance. With the other awards in hand and meeting the criteria, I thought I had a good shot. And if I did get this award, I figured, buyers would have to seriously consider the dolls.

In January 2011, the Toy Association announced the finalists on its website. The awards would be presented to the winners at the annual gala known as the "Oscars" of the toy industry during Toy Fair. Excited, hopeful, and crossing my fingers, I opened the Toy Association award page scrolled down to the "Girl Toy of the Year" section…and the Go! Go! Sports Girls were not selected. Disappointed, I read the list of finalists:

- Barbie Video Girl by Mattel
- FurReal Friends GOGO, My Walkin' Pup by Hasbro, Inc.

- Justin Bieber Music Video Collection Singing Figures by The Bridge Direct, Inc.
- Monster High Doll Assortment by Mattel
- Princess & Me 18" Dolls by Jakks Pacific, Inc.
- Zoobles Single Pack by Spin Master Ltd
- Squinkies Cupcake Surprize! Bake Shop by Blip Toys

I thought, wait a minute! These are all toys produced by large toy companies. There was not one small company on this list and most of these products reinforced harmful stereotypes. I was curious, what was nominated for the "Boy Toy of the Year"?

- Air Hogs Hawk Eye by Spin Master Ltd
- NERF N-Strike Stampede ECS Blaster by Hasbro, Inc.
- Hot Wheels RC Stealth Rides by Mattel
- Real Construction Deluxe Workshop by Jakks Pacific, Inc.
- Spy Net Video Watch by Jakks Pacific, Inc.
- *Toy Story 3* Blast Off Buzz Lightyear by Thinkway Toys
- TRON: Legacy Zero Gravity Light Cycle by Disney and Spin Master

As Global Toy Expert, Richard Gottlieb writes, "Who assigned the toy industry the responsibility of telling boys and girls with which toys they are allowed to play?"[1] I was noticing how the toy industry fueled gender stereotypes. I wondered why small companies were not selected and if the awards were only for the larger companies. Most of all, I wondered how can an industry that should encourage creativity, innovation, and uniqueness be so archaic and antiquated?

Curious, I went back to the list of 2010 finalists and saw the same players, just different products. Barbie Fashionistas by Mattel, Moxie Girlz Art-titude Doll, and BFC Ink Doll both by MGA Entertainment among others were on the list of Girl Toys, and Matchbox Rocky the Robot Truck by Mattel, and Nerf N-Strike Raider Rapid Fire CS-35 and Transformers Construction Devastator both by Hasbro were on the Boy Toy list. I went back to 2009, 2008, 2007 and found the same pattern. The same big toy companies. The same gender stereotyped toys.

I was beginning to understand that feeling of disparity I had between the praise I was hearing from parents and the lack of orders from toy buyers. The US market size for the total toy industry is approximately $27 billion annually, and buyers are looking for a big piece of that, but they are all looking in the same basket for the next Barbie or G.I. Joe. They are overlooking the small players who may have the most creative, innovative, and unique new products.

Ironically, in 2011 the Campaign for a Commercial-Free Childhood announced their popular TOADY

---

1   Richard Gottlieb, "Boys' Toys, Girls' Toys and the TOTY Awards" (Global Toy News, February 20, 2016).

Awards (Toys Oppressive and Destructive to Young Children), and the Monster High dolls had made the list. They had made the list of the best toy of the year and the worst toy of the year. How can that be? TOADY described the dolls as, "So many damaging sexualized stereotypes into one creepy package. Behold the horrors of impossibly thin body types; recoil from the micro-miniskirts, booty shorts, and fishnet stockings; shriek in frustration, because—in Mattel's world—girls are always relegated to the sidelines."[2] My vote: Worst toy of the year!

In 2016, Salem State University professor of media and communications, Rebecca Hains, blasted the Toy Association in a *Washington Post* article titled, "Boys play with dolls, and girls play with spaceships. Someone tell the toy makers." She wrote, "The 'Boy Toy of the Year' and the 'Girl Toy of the Year'—will rely upon and reinforce the outdated gender stereotyping of toys."[3] Dan Nessel, founder of DadDoes.com also challenged the industry at this same time and launched a Change.org petition to end the boy and girl awards. The Toy Association listened and retired the boy and girl toy awards in 2017.

The TOTY award categories may have changed, but everything else is pretty much the same. Products by large toy companies are preferred by risk-averse toy buyers,

2   Josh Golin, "Vote Now for Worst Toy of the Year" (HuffPost, December 7, 2017), https://www.huffpost.com/entry/vote-now-for-worst-toy-of_b_1093194.

3   Rebecca Hains, "Boys Play with Dolls, and Girls Play with Spaceships. Someone Tell the Toy Makers. - The Washington Post" (The Washington Post, February 12, 2016), https://www.washingtonpost.com/posteverything/wp/2016/02/12/boys-play-with-dolls-and-girls-play-with-spaceships-someone-tell-the-toy-makers/.

and gender stereotypes continue to be fueled. The 2019 and 2020 Doll of the Year award went to L.O.L. Surprise! O.M.G. Fashion Dolls by MGA Entertainment, which are yet another line of sexy fashion dolls with names similar to Ty Girlz: Honeylicious, Bhad Gurl, Groovy Babe, and Swag to name a few. Again, just because a large toy company launches a new product doesn't make it a good product.

My battle was becoming clear, and my determination to fight and win was becoming fierce.

CHAPTER 17

DISRUPTING THE PINK AISLE

"My coach said I run like a girl.
And I said if he ran a little faster, he could too."
– Mia Hamm

Before Toy Fair 2012, I worked to restructure the doll line to make it more appealing to buyers. Soccer Girl Cassie, Gymnastics Girl Maya, and Dancer Girl M.C. were top sellers, but I discontinued my two lowest selling dolls. I only sold about a hundred Golfer Girl Brooke dolls and seventy-five Softball Girl Samantha dolls. I was surprised and tried hard to market and sell both. There was interest from the United States Golf Association, but not enough for them to place an order. I managed to get them in golf pro shops, but they didn't sell well there. Softball Girl was harder to market, and I found it difficult to find outlets to sell them.

I added four new dolls—Cheerleader Girl Roxy, Volleyball Girl Steph, Basketball Girl Kate, and Soccer Girl Anna—to launch at Toy Fair 2012. I had enough soccer research to know a second soccer doll would sell. My goal from the beginning was to add diversity to the line, but it was costly due to the amount of fabric I needed to buy. I already had Basketball Girl Taye with darker skin but knew this was my opportunity to add a second dark-skin doll, Soccer Girl Anna, in a sport that was one of my top sellers.

I wanted to do this even though Basketball Girl Taye was not selling well, which didn't make sense because basketball was one of the most popular and fastest growing sports for girls. When I launched the dolls in 2009, I had good interest from the WNBA, and they liked the diversity. They were supportive but didn't have a big budget and never placed an order. The buyers at Toy Fair, however, were dismissive of Taye, telling me, "Black dolls don't sell well."

The company most known for offering diversity in their doll line is American Girl, but in 2014 they discontinued two racially diverse dolls—one Black and one Asian. There was a storm of complaints, but the company stood by their choice, stating it was a purely business-led decision.[1]

I didn't agree with the toy buyers' feedback on Taye. I believe kids should have a choice between skin tones as much as a choice between a sports doll and fashion doll. I ignored their advice and added Soccer Girl Anna. And because I believed basketball was popular enough to work, I added a light-skin basketball doll named Kate.

A few small stores picked up both soccer dolls, Cassie and Anna, but Anna sold better online. Overall, Soccer

---

1   Annabel Fenwick Elliott, "American Girl Forced to Defend Decision to Discontinue Two Racially Diverse Dolls Following Furious Storm of Complaints" (Daily Mail Online, May 28, 2014), https://www.dailymail.co.uk/femail/article-2640831/American-Girl-forced-defend-decision-discontinue-two-racially-diverse-dolls-following-furious-storm-complaints.html.

Girl Anna sold better than Basketball Girl Taye, but Basketball Girl Kate did better than Taye.

Years later, in 2018, I was speaking at the Girl Empowerment Network in Austin, Texas, and led a breakout session with some twenty-five girls between ages eight and fourteen. I brought a mix of Cheerleader Girl Roxy, Runner Girl Ella, Basketball Girl Taye, and Soccer Girl Anna. I told the girls they could pick out any doll they wanted. Not one of the Black girls picked the Black dolls. Only one white girl picked a Black doll. That was it.

Unknowingly, I was doing my own "doll test," and sadly the results were the same. The famous "doll test" was conducted by Mamie Phipps Clark, PhD and Kenneth Clark, PhD, a husband-and-wife team of social psychologists, on children in the 1930s and 1940s. Black children were placed in a room with two dolls before them—one Black and one white and were asked a series of questions: *Which doll is pretty? Which doll is ugly? Which doll is bad? Which doll is good? Which doll do you want to play with?* Overwhelmingly, the Black children showed a preference for dolls with white skin. The Clarks concluded that even before the Black children could fully articulate their feelings about race, they were already damaged by a sense of inferiority. Over the past few years, several psychologists and news organizations have tried to replicate the tests. The results often remained the same.[2]

---

2   Ernie Suggs, "How Mamie and Kenneth Clark Used Dolls to Overturn School Segregation Laws" (The Atlanta Journal-Constitution, January 24, 2020), https://www.ajc.com/news/martin-luther-king-jr/black-doll-white-doll-and-racial-shame-thats-nothing-to-play-with/KPFSRBF5PZHKPLDNMKXMYZXZIA/.

Similarly, this was pointed out by Sujata Luther, a seasoned veteran of the toy industry, holding top positions during her tenure at Mattel, MGA Entertainment, and Nickelodeon, and former President of Just Play. Throughout her career she has studied children and said:

> At the age of 3 or 5, a Barbie is put in front of girls in a hugely sexy outfit, Caucasian, with big blonde hair and it's the idea of perfect beauty. A lot of things have changed the last 10 years, but I've gone to countries like Africa where we've put many, many skin tones in front of children, African children, and they migrate to the white doll saying, that's what I look like. Much about dolls is what you want to look like versus what you are.

> I've spent a lot of time in Japan trying to understand how to make dolls appealing to little Japanese kids. All Japanese icons, be it a cartoon character, an animal character, a doll, they all have round eyes. Think about that. I did and we did a study in Japan, and I hired psychologists to try and explain this whole phenomenon and it's all about what we have at five-years-old. For the test, we put all these different looking Barbie dolls in front of the kids, and they automatically went for the dolls with round eyes. It's no wonder the number one plastic surgery in Japan is the eyelid.

> There's this whole thing about being happy and proud of who you are, while striving for this ideal of beauty, but the ideal of beauty, unfortunately, is

the Caucasian model. I grew up in India. Nobody wanted an Indian dark skin doll. Everyone wanted that blonde hair doll, including me.

This illustrates how kids pick up on cultural stereotypes and begin to show bias at an early age. According to Danielle Perszyk, a psychologist as Northwestern University, "not only do children absorb the stereotypes they see, but they also become increasingly attuned to social category labels, social status, and the biases exhibited by family members."[3]

Toy buyers are certainly risk-averse, *and* predominately white, *and* many are put in the "toy buying" position not knowing or caring about the toy industry's social and developmental impact. What I hope the Toy Association can soon offer is a program to teach new buyers the importance of diversity and inclusion in toys.

According to Anne Marie Kehoe, Walmart's former vice president of toys, understanding the play of children and the ability to rethink merchandise starts with retail leadership and retail buyers. She explains:

"Within retail leadership, somebody really needs to understand and encourage the worth of diversity and innovation. Toys are unique and different. I started in the beauty category, and you could go through Vogue magazine or the internet to see the trends. You can't do that in toys. In toys, you

---

3   Amanda Armstrong, "Bias Starts as Early as Preschool, but Can Be Unlearned" (Edutopia, June 4, 2019), https://www.edutopia.org/article/bias-starts-early-preschool-can-be-unlearned/.

must think about the parents, caregivers, and kids. Insight is so important in this industry."

"It's important for new buyers to understand the responsibility of being a toy buyer in a different way than just the responsibility of buying another category, because it's very emotional. There are certain sensitivities. A toy buyer has the responsibility to choose what to bring to the shelf. There isn't a website that toy buyers can go to get updated insights, to learn what do, what to ask suppliers, or what to look for. It takes a lot of time and an emotional connection and on top of that, toys must be fun. And just like anything, it needs to become a part of the fabric of a buying team."

A slightly less controversial addition to the line was a cheerleading doll, a sport that had fought for years to get recognition. I'll admit, it took me awhile to come around on this, having grown up preferring to be on the field or court than cheering on the sidelines. Times have changed. These young women and men are talented athletes whose competitions deserve respect and recognition. There are some 3.82 million cheerleaders in the United States, of which 97 percent are female.[4] In 1997 cheerleading was recognized as an independent sport, but it wasn't met with official approval until 1999.[5] I added Cheerleader

---

4   Valerie Ninemire, "What Are Some Surprising Facts about Cheerleading History?" (LiveAbout, January 4, 2019), https://www.liveabout.com/cheerleading-history-4080643.

5   "Cheerleading History" (Epic Sports, n.d.), https://cheer.epicsports.com/cheerleading-stunts-history.html.

Girl Roxy after my dear friend, Roxanne, one of my personal cheerleaders.

Adding Volleyball Girl was an emotional decision, which came from my heart and not research. Probably not the wisest business decision, and at the time, volleyball wasn't a big sport for girls under ten years old, but I added her to the line after my good friend Steph, who at age forty-two was diagnosed with stage 2 breast cancer. It was shocking news for her and everyone close to her because she was super healthy and a great athlete, having played volleyball at Northwestern University in the late '80s. I wanted to design Volleyball Girl Steph in a purple and white uniform in honor of my dear friend. (Fourteen years later, Steph is healthy and well!)

I was excited to return to Toy Fair 2012 with new products and as an experienced vendor. My good friend Erica offered to help me. Like Toni, she is outgoing, fun, and a passionate Go! Go! Sports Girls salesperson. Erica was one of the first people I talked to about my idea, so she was familiar with the dolls and concept and had been involved in a few of my projects. In fact, Dancer Girl M.C. is named after her daughter.

Erica is also the voice for the Go! Go! Sports Girls video. In 2009, Keith and his marketing team offered to create a video. We needed a narrator, and I enthusiastically told Keith I could do it. He paused and looked at me like he was trying to figure out how to break the news to me kindly. He proceeded to tell me I have a nice voice, but it's a bit nasally. Whatever! I'm from the Midwest. I had heard this before, so I agreed to look for someone else and dropped any dreams I had to become a voice actor.

When I shared this story with Erica, we both had a good laugh, and she said, "Hey, I'll give it a shot." She did a great job. Once the video went live, I had people email me and ask, "How did you get Katie Couric to narrate the video?"

At Toy Fair 2012, I had even more media attention. The word was out, and people were hearing about the Go! Go! Sports Girls and liked that I was disrupting the pink aisles. They wanted to know more. I was hearing their stories too. Many women told me they were frustrated with the products marketed to their girls and would never allow Barbie and Bratz dolls into their home.

Mixing up the doll line seemed to have worked since I was busier than I had ever been meeting with toy buyers. Erica and I spent all day sharing the doll line with a steady stream of people. During one of those busy moments, I noticed one young woman waiting outside my booth. She was patient and waited for a lull before approaching me. She smiled and said, "Hi, I'm Debbie Sterling, and I've been researching you and love your girl empowerment product. I'm an engineer, and I am creating a girl empowerment engineering toy. I was hoping you could help me."

The following year Debbie launched GoldieBlox, a construction toy for girls encouraging STEM (science, technology, engineering, and math.) Initially, she heard similar antiquated remarks that I heard from toy industry professionals: *"Construction toys for girls will never catch on, and 'fighting nature' is no good." "Girls like dolls and princesses, they don't like building."* She knew this was incorrect and started a Kickstarter campaign in 2012 that raised nearly $300 thousand. She became a force in the toy industry and burst into the market after winning a contest run by Intuit, scoring herself a commercial that aired during Super Bowl 2014. We encouraged and supported each other as we disrupted the pink aisle and challenged gender stereotypes.

Years later, Debbie told me, "The first time we met at Toy Fair, I was walking around Javits with the GoldieBlox prototype trying to talk to as many people as I could for advice. You were the only person there that was excited about what I was doing. You understood it and thought it was a big idea. Most of the people at Toy Fair did not get it; they looked at me, and they looked at the idea, and they thought, "Okay, this is some niche idea that could sit in the back of an education supply store gathering dust." Nobody there thought it had mainstream viability or potential. And almost everybody I talked to, besides you, was trying to talk me out of continuing; telling me it's a huge uphill battle, and you have to raise all this money. It's so hard.

"I decided NO, this needs to exist. Girls deserve this. I see this as the Dora the Explorer of STEM. I will climb the mountain because if that's what needs to be done to have this exist and be in the world, then so be it. So, I thought, all right, bring it on!"

Little did we know, our changemaker team was growing. In 2012, Bettina Chen and Alice Brooks, recent Stanford University engineering grads launched Roominate, a girl-oriented construction kit including circuits that can be wired. Also, that year Ian Harkin and Lucie Follett launched Lottie Dolls encouraging kids to follow their dreams. In 2014, Julie Kerwin launched I am Elemental, the first-ever female action figures. Also in 2014, Laurel Wider launched Wonder Crew, a line of dolls for boys encouraging social-emotional skill building—because wanting to nurture and connect is simply human, not gender specific.

At the time we did not know one another, but we were like-minded and fed up with the toys marketed to children. We were determined to challenge the status quo, the patriarchal toy industry, and create change. We were looking for ways to get noticed and stand out from the mainstream products and behemoth toy companies. Despite all our individual roadblocks that came from toy buyers, we were seeing success thanks to demand from parents.

Julie Kerwin was told by a buyer that girls don't play with action figures, and he suggested she model the dolls after Polly Pockets. He continued with his advice and told her that she needed to "dumb it down" (you heard me right!) because kids wouldn't understand female action figures that celebrate superpower characteristics such as persistence, bravery, and honesty. Julie's goal was to show children that all the superpowers they could ever want or need are already inside of them and to encourage girls to create their own "save the world" storylines.

Julie did not take his advice and started a Kickstarter campaign that was fully funded in forty-eight hours, but she noticed something unexpected. Men were buying the I am Elemental action figures for their daughters. Fathers and grandfathers, who spent their entire childhoods playing with action figures, were excited about sharing this experience with their daughters and granddaughters.

Laurel Wider said, "Buyers were confused with the concept of boys and dolls or boys and nurturing play. Wonder Crew began as a grassroots movement. Parents and influencers immediately understood and rallied behind Wonder Crew. They saw the play gap and ultimately made the line a success."

And Ian Harkin, after losing two major accounts due to copyright infringement, the *Guardian* did a full-page feature on Lottie Dolls. "After the article was released, a large percentage of independent toy stores owned and run by women, knew what we were trying to do, and they bought Lottie immediately. Having people believe in you and support you is the biggest reward." Ian said.

At Toy Fair 2012, the Go! Go! Sports Girls were once again named one of 'The Coolest Toys," this time by *Parents* Magazine. Two years in a row the Go! Go! Sports Girls received awards by two large publications, and still toy buyers were hesitant. But this did lead to large orders from non-toy buyers. One from USA Gymnastics and an "Iron Girl" doll for the World Triathlon Corporation.

I decided I needed to work harder to get my story out to the public. The reaction to my product was always enthusiastic, so if I could build consumer demand, I might be able to exert more pressure on toy buyers. I researched public relations firms, but most were too expensive. I liked one small firm in Chicago, and I would have hired them, but the owner called me one day and said, "I've been thinking about what we could do for your company. In all honesty, I don't think we can accomplish what you have done. You are doing a great job, and I don't think you should or need to pay for our services."

I appreciated her honesty, especially the vote of confidence from a fellow businesswoman, but I still needed contacts, emails, and phone numbers. I hired an online platform service called Meltwater, a company that develops and markets media monitoring and had contacts. I began another media blitz in May, and this time I included national talk shows — *The Today Show*, *Good Morning America*, *CBS This Morning*, *Fox & Friends*, and more.

With the momentum I felt after Toy Fair, encouragement from Kara, and my determination to stand out and create change, I also decided to apply for the fifth season of *Shark Tank*, which would air in late 2013. It was a popular show, and people were constantly asking, "Have you ever thought of going on *Shark Tank*?"

After filling out and submitting the lengthy online application, I quickly received a phone call from the casting director. She said she really liked my idea and had never heard of anything like it. I had made it to the next round, and in the next few weeks, they would make their final casting decision.

I was quick to get to work. *Shark Tank* required a five-minute video pitch, and Keith and his team offered to help, so it looked professional. I was excited because being on *Shark Tank* would give me the exposure I needed. The casting director told me I had a good chance, and I submitted a great video. I was optimistic and started preparing for my pitch to the Sharks. I asked Kara to join me on the show if I made it. I pictured the two of us in the *Shark Tank* waiting area that looked like an aquarium and wondered which Shark would invest. I was confident… until I received a rejection letter. I quickly emailed the casting director, and she explained it was a tough decision and invited me to apply for the sixth season.

Feeling defeated again, I knew what to do. I had to stand up straight, raise my chin, and move forward. That I continued to always get close had to mean something.

CHAPTER 18

BRAVE GIRLS

"Surround yourself only with people
who are going to take you higher."
– Oprah Winfrey

I have been asked the question many times, "What did you do before you started the Go! Go! Sports Girls brand?" My answer is, "I was a mom to three small children." Most often the reaction is surprise, like I should at least have been a CEO at a large toy company or high-level executive before launching my own toy company, not *just* a mom. I have learned no one should ever underestimate the power of a mother.

Having children made me more aware of where inequities begin, even as I saw my sons and daughter as equals. At first, I thought media and the products marketed for them, did too: they were sweet, innocent, and educational—*Sesame Street*, *Dora the Explorer*, *Blues Clues*, *The Very Hungry Caterpillar*, *Goodnight Moon*, stuffed animals, baby dolls, puzzles, you get the point—all equally relevant and appealing to my sons and daughter.

But when Peter was eight and Grace was six, I started to notice a discrepancy in how media, books, and products marketed to kids. Products marketed to girls were associated with appearance and attractiveness, and products marketed to boys were associated with violence and aggression. My boys were not violent or aggressive, and I didn't want to encourage this, and I didn't want my smart daughter to feel pressure to focus on her appearance.

One of my first observations of this was at a toy store in the spring of 2002. I wanted to buy a science kit for my kids and was immediately annoyed with what I found. There was a boy science aisle and a girl science aisle. I wondered when science became gender specific, but I followed directions and went down the "boy" science aisle where I found many great science kits. The one that caught my eye was an exploding volcano. The cover of the packaging showed two boys wearing safety goggles laughing as the volcano exploded into the air. I thought to myself, "good option, good *outdoor* option!"

I was curious, what science kits were marketed to girls? I went down the "girl" science aisle. The shelves were filled with pink packaged science kits with a common theme: Yes, girls, you can be a scientist and make your own fingernail polish, lip balm, perfume, bath gel, lotion, face mask, shampoo, makeup, jewelry, or headband. It was all associated with appearance!

With gender inequality on my radar now I could see how it could affect my daughter. I remembered the dumb blonde comments from my teachers and peers in middle school, and I didn't want this to become her experience. I was not about to dismiss these small moments that could potentially have a big and negative impact on her social and emotional development.

I have received comments over the years telling me I'm overreacting because kids don't pick up on stereotypes. "It's just a doll," or "it's just a science kit," people say. But over and over studies show children pick up on stereotypes at a very young age. A 2017 study by Andrei Cimpian and Sarah-Jane Leslie found that by age six, young girls are less likely than boys to view their own gender as brilliant, and girls start to believe that specific activities are "not for them," simply because they think they're not smart enough.

Their research suggests that American children are picking up on cultural stereotypes about brilliance at an early age. Unfortunately, these stereotypes suggest that girls aren't as smart as boys. Books, movies, and TV shows often promote the cultural stereotype that being intellectually gifted is a male quality. Research suggests that these stereotypes may have lasting effects that guide girls interests away from things that they perceive as not for them and can significantly limit a girl's full potential and happiness by ignoring who they truly are in order to "fit in" to what society expects of them.[1]

That day in the toy aisle those expectations were clear. As a parent and consumer, I was seeing how the toy industry was limiting children by limiting their choices, which is bad enough. What's more, marketing decisions such as this have deeper implications. A burgeoning scientist may feel the need to unnecessarily spend social capital bucking cultural norms and emotional energy resisting the ques-

---

1   Andrei Cimpian and Sarah-Jane Leslie, "Why Young Girls Don't Think They Are Smart Enough" (The New York Times, January 26, 2017), https://www.nytimes.com/2017/01/26/well/family/why-young-girls-dont-think-they-are-smart-enough.html.

tion—explicit or implicit—of whether or not she belongs just to pursue her dreams.

Claire Shipman and Katty Kay, authors of *The Confidence Code for Girls* surveyed more than 1,300 girls from ages eight to eighteen and their parents. They found between ages eight and fourteen, girls' confidence levels fall by 30 percent. At fourteen, when girls are hitting their low, boys' confidence is still 27 percent higher. And the effects can be long lasting.[2] This is not surprising with the confusing and conflicting messages girls receive. We need to understand the undercurrent of subtle and overt messages and images that contribute and fuel the declining self-confidence of girls at a young age. That's why I push back when I hear "It's just a science kit."

According to Merriam-Webster, *confidence* is a feeling or consciousness of one's powers or of reliance on one's circumstances. Confidence is a belief in one's ability with or without the conditions to back up future success. For one person, their education and experience might instill confidence in a certain endeavor while someone else might believe in their potential for success simply because they have no reason not to. However, confidence has been socialized to mean aggressive and loud, and sometimes people try to conform, which can be mistaken for confidence. Confidence isn't having a big ego or bullying others. Confidence comes from understanding your strengths and values.

---

2   Claire Shipman, Katty Kay, and Jillellyn Riley, "The Confidence Gap for Girls: 5 Tips for Parents of Tween and Teen Girls" (The New York Times, October 1, 2018), https://www.nytimes.com/2018/10/01/well/family/confidence-gap-teen-girls-tips-parents.html.

What Toy Fair 2012 showed me is that others were feeling the way I was about the toy industry. Others who were also moved to act.

In 2013 Melissa Atkins Wardy, owner of Pigtail Pals & Ballcap Buddies, organized The Brave Girls Alliance, a powerhouse think-tank and advocacy group of girl empowerment experts. They asked me to be a part of it, along with an all-star cast of women, including *New York Times* bestselling author Peggy Orenstein; parenting expert and *New York Times* bestselling author Rachel Simmons; producer, writer, director, and co-director of Pixar's *Brave* Brenda Chapman; Nancy Gruver, founder and CEO of New Moon Girl Media; and children's media culture expert, professor, and author Rebecca Hains, among others. Our goal was to ask media creators to expand their version of what it means to be a girl and recognize girls as whole, complex people and not as gender stereotypes. On October 11, 2013, the second International Day of the Girl Child, we planned a "Take Back Media Times Square" campaign kick-off.

We had women and a few men working in all corners of the world to promote our campaign. In New York we arranged a press conference, interviews, and through a crowdsourcing fundraising campaign, we raised enough money from supporters to rent a digital billboard in Times Square to broadcast messages from girls and people around the world wanting a better, more diverse, and non-sexualized media representation of girls. It was exciting to see empowering, larger-than-life messages from individuals all over the world light up the evening sky on the corner of Seventh Avenue and 43rd Street.

"#BraveGirlsWant media creators to rethink products in development and ensure they teach girls to be strong, intelligent, and adventurous."

"#BraveGirlsWant to be America's next president, not Top Model."

#BraveGirlsWant stories with girls like them at the center, not on the fringes as supporting roles."

#BraveGirlsWant to be able to stand up for themselves without being called names, told to 'be a lady,' or feeling shame."

The Brave Girls Alliance went on to push media and retailers to do a better job representing girls for two more years, but we eventually hit expensive roadblocks that prevented us from moving forward. I am proud of our accomplishments and honored to have worked with strong, smart, brave, and fierce women. We rose together and created change. I realized what I had known all along—there is power in the pack, and I have always had a fierce pack.

New York Times bestselling author and US Soccer Olympic Gold Medalist Abby Wambach wrote in her book, *Wolfpack*, "Whether you're a mom, a college student, a CEO, or little girl, you need a crew of brave and honest women to support you. You need them to hold you accountable to your greatness, remind you of who you are, and join you to change the world."[3]

---

3   Abby Wambach, *Wolfpack: How to Come Together, Unleash Our Power, and Change the Game (New York: Celadon Books, 2019).*

Study after study shows women who support women are more successful in business and in life. "Such an inner circle can provide trustworthy, gender-relevant information about job cultures and social support, which are very important to women in male-dominated settings," said Yang Yang, a research assistant professor at Northwestern's Kellogg School of Management. [4]

I knew I had come as far as I had because of my pack from women like Ina who mentored me to women like Debbie who I was mentoring. Roxanne, Toni, Kara, Steph, Erica, Christy, and many more brave and honest women who supported me and joined me to change the world.

My pack gave me strength, but I was beginning to feel defeat that the enthusiasm from parents and the media for my mission-driven product wasn't translating into sales from toy buyers. During a heart-to-heart with Steve, he said, "Maybe you're ahead of your time. Maybe our culture isn't ready for your product." That felt true in the moment, but I wanted to be brave. I wanted to pull my pack together because I knew girls deserved more.

4   Kayla Stoner, "Most Successful Women Surround Themselves with Other Women" (Northwestern Now, January 22, 2019), https://news.northwestern.edu/stories/2019/01/most-successful-women-surround-themselves-with-other-women/#:~:text=Women%20who%20communicate%20regularly%20with,the%20University%20of%20Notre%20Dame.

PART 3

○ ○

Dream Big, Go for It, and Don't Give Up

CHAPTER 19

BOOST FROM A BELIEVER

"Like any artist without an art form,
she became dangerous."
— *Toni Morrison*

During my 2012 media blitz, I sent an email to Gretchen Carlson, the *Fox & Friends* host. I found her to be strong, smart, confident, and she had an edge, which I liked.

On May 3, 2012 at 10:27 a.m., I sent an email to Gretchen.

Five minutes later, at 10:32 a.m., I received a reply. "Hi Jodi! Thanks for the email. A *Fox & Friends* producer will be reaching out to you! GC."

I was thrilled, and wow, that was quick. At 1:57 p.m. I received an email from a producer, and on May 11, 2012 the Go! Go! Sports Girls were featured on *Fox & Friends* in a segment titled, "Sports Dolls Inspire Girls to Dream Big."

Throughout the year, Gretchen and I stayed in contact. We were like-minded and strong advocates for women and girls. I emailed Gretchen with an idea to have me on her show during Toy Fair 2013 to showcase innovative girl empowerment products. She agreed, and on February 11, I was scheduled to be on *Fox & Friends* during the 7:00 a.m. hour, in a segment titled, "Innovative Toys that

Help Girls Stay Mentally and Physically Fit," featuring the Go! Go! Sports Girls, GoldieBlox, Kaskey Kids, and Roominate.

Needing to be at Fox Studio at 6:30 a.m., I woke up at 4:30 a.m. excited and nervous about going on live national TV. At 6:00 a.m., as I walked out the hotel lobby to catch a cab, my phone rang. It was the producer, Samantha, from *Fox & Friends*. She explained to me that they needed to cancel my segment because Pope Benedict XVI announced his resignation. The last time a Pope had resigned was 500 years ago, and this was a big story.

All I could think was, *Really? A pope hasn't stepped down in 500 years, and it has to happen today? I got bumped by the pope? Rotten luck!* Later that day my luck turned, and Samantha emailed me saying they rescheduled my segment for 7:40 a.m. on the twelfth.

Getting up early the next morning, still excited and nervous, I jumped in a cab praying for no natural disasters or big world news and headed to the studio. Upon arrival, I was escorted to makeup and hair before stepping onto the stage. Gretchen smiled, and things were moving quickly, so there was no time for introductions or small talk. The segment was the last one, so it was short and sweet. Once we were off camera, I thanked Gretchen, and as I was escorted off the stage, she touched my arm and said, "Do you have a few more minutes? I would like to feature you on our After the Show segment." This was five additional minutes of airtime.

Soon after my appearance on *Fox & Friends*, Gretchen announced her departure as host of the morning show to launch her new afternoon program on *Fox* called, "The

Real Story with Gretchen Carlson." She asked me to be part of her Female Power Panel. I was flattered and honored, and I proceeded to be on her show four times before she left *Fox News* in 2016, turning the network upside down on her way out.

I loved being on Gretchen's show, but my favorite segment with her was on October 11, 2013.

I reached out to Gretchen to let her know I would be in town for the campaign launch of Brave Girls Alliance, and she invited me on the show to help promote my cause and to celebrate International Day of the Girl Child. An hour before I arrived at Fox Studio, I received a call from a producer saying, "Gretchen was wondering if you would come on air makeup free along with her to empower girls and discuss raising empowered young women in a 'sex sells' culture." I loved the idea! I never wear a lot of makeup, I always thought *Fox* makeup and hair was over the top, and I really don't care, so without hesitation, I agreed.

Gretchen started the segment saying, "For the first time in cable news, here I am, makeup free as is my guest today, Jodi Norgaard." This sentence struck me, and so many thoughts started going through my head. *This is crazy that it's a big deal for two women to appear on television without makeup. Perfection is constantly forced upon women. It would never be a big deal for two men to appear on television sans makeup. Gretchen is challenging the system right here and right now, and I'm proud she asked me to do it with her.*

Alicia Keys famously said, "I don't want to cover up anymore. Not my face, not my mind, not my soul, not my thoughts, not my dreams, not my struggles, not my emotional growth. Nothing." Gretchen was doing exactly that while preparing to share her truth with the world. I was proud to be part of her journey.

Gretchen and I are still connected, and I admire her for her strength, bravery, courage, kindness, and fierceness. By leaving Fox, filing a sexual harassment complaint against *Fox News* chairman Roger Ailes, and risking her career, she became a pillar in the #MeToo movement. She continues to advocate and fight for the advancement of women and women's rights through her nonprofit, Lift Our Voices, dedicated to ending forced arbitration and NDAs. She was also instrumental in passing the Ending Forced Arbitration of Sexual Assault and Sexual Harassment Act of 2021. Her career is so inspiring and powerful that it was portrayed in a Showtime miniseries, *The Loudest Voice*, and the film, *Bombshell*...and I'm more than a little proud that our makeup-free segment was portrayed in both.

CHAPTER 20

RUNNING INTO WALMART

"The little things?
The little moments? They aren't little."
— *Jon Kabat-Zinn*

After five years and what felt like 500 rejections, I decided to give Toy Fair one more shot in 2013. I told Steve that if I had little or no success, it would be my last Toy Fair, and I would throw in the towel. That was a hard, gut-wrenching realization.

That year I decided to head to Toy Fair alone, and I wasn't nearly as optimistic or enthusiastic as I had been in previous years. I didn't rent a booth because it was too expensive, and it wasn't cost effective. When I told Christy Kaskey my plan, she said, "Why don't you set up your dolls in my booth and hang out with me?" I was grateful for her kind offer and support and gladly accepted.

Over the years, I developed relationships with buyers from small and medium specialty stores, including independent brick and mortar stores and Learning Express as well as large retailers like Toys R Us, Target, Barnes & Noble, Amazon, and Walmart.com. The Go! Go! Sports Girls were on all the large retailers' online stores, but the big orders came from having your product in big-box stores, and this was my last shot.

During Toy Fair, I always forced myself to network because I needed to know people in the industry. It wasn't easy because after a long day of standing and small talk, the last thing I wanted to do in the evenings was more standing and small talk. A quiet hotel room with room service was always what I preferred, but I persisted and dug deep to find the courage and energy to walk alone into a room full of people who seemed to know each other.

One of my favorite networking groups was Women in Toys, a community that champions the advancement of women through leadership, networking, and educational opportunities. I had met their president, Joan Packard-Luks, who was a partner at The ThinkTank Emporium, an intellectual property coaching and consulting group. She wanted to champion the advancement of the Go! Go! Sports Girls, and I wanted to champion the advancement of Women in Toys. I loved their mission, and they were all about women supporting women.

At Toy Fair I signed up to attend one of their educational opportunities about getting your product on Walmart shelves, which was exactly what I wanted to learn. It was held in the morning in a conference room in the lowest level of the Javits Center, and getting there felt like a labyrinth of passages and secret chambers. Running late and trying to navigate the maze, I finally made it to the packed room of approximately one hundred people and found an empty seat toward the back of the room.

At the front of the room was a panel of six Walmart toy buyers who answered questions and offered suggestions and strategies to get your product on store shelves. I felt like I was back in college writing frantically and taking pages of notes. I learned that one of the panelists, Seth, was the girl toy buyer, and I wanted to meet him. At the close of the conference, Seth thanked us for coming and said, "Now we will start the five-minute pitches for those who signed up."

Wait! Pitches? For those who signed up? How could I have missed this? Had I known, I would have taken advantage of this opportunity. That was the kind of opportunity I desperately needed. Without thinking, my hand shot up. (I'm so glad I found the confidence to raise my hand again.)

"Excuse me? Do you have times available if you didn't sign up to pitch your product?" I said.

"I don't think so, but if anyone would like to meet me here at 4:00 p.m., after the scheduled pitches are completed, I will let you know if there are additional times," Seth replied. *I am so doing this.* I thought. *I am not going to miss out on an opportunity to pitch to Walmart.*

At 3:45 p.m., I started making my way back to the conference room. I went through this maze before, so I was confident...until I got lost. With my dolls, notepad, pen, and business cards in hand, I started to panic and asked people for directions.. I looked at my watch and only had three minutes to figure it out. At exactly 4:00 p.m. I saw the conference room and quickly picked up my pace, sweating and worried I had missed my chance when, as I turned the corner to enter the room, BAM! I ran straight into Seth. Literally ran straight into Seth! My dolls, notebook, pen, business cards—everything—flew through the air and landed on the ground.

Trying to keep my composure while kneeling down to pick up my things off the floor, I looked up at him and said, "I'm so sorry I ran into you. Are you okay? You're the person I wanted to see. Do you still have time for me to pitch my product?"

He laughed and said, "You made quite an entrance," as he bent down to help me. "Sure, I'll listen to your pitch, but I can't do it today. How about tomorrow at 9:30 a.m.? I'll come to your booth." Thrilled, I jotted down Christy's booth number on one of my business cards and thanked him.

Even though I was excited Seth agreed to an appointment, I knew I faced a timing issue. That was the morning I was supposed to have been on *Fox & Friends* with Gretchen but was bumped by the pope and was now scheduled for 7:40 a.m. the next morning. Could I meet with Seth less than two hours later? I knew I had to figure it out. I had to make it work.

On my way back to Christy's booth, I ran into a few people I knew and shared my exciting news. Their response wasn't what I was expecting. They told me not to meet with the Walmart buyers and that I was crazy to consider it because Walmart is known for chewing up small companies and spitting them out. They told me they would ruin my business. I disagreed. I saw an opportunity, and if nothing else, Seth would provide helpful feedback. Limiting my options wasn't progress, and I was ready to move forward.

That evening, I sent Gretchen's producer an email explaining my timing issue, so she arranged a car to pick me up at the studio and race me back to the Javits Center after my interview. Traffic was heavy, but by 9:20 a.m. I was in Christy's booth ready for my meeting with Seth. Fifteen minutes passed. I patiently stood at the edge of Christy's booth quietly practicing my pitch. Thirty minutes passed, and I was starting to think he wasn't coming.

Then at 10:00 a.m. I saw Seth walking toward me accompanied by two women. My heart started beating fast. Christy looked at me and said, "You've got this. Good luck."

First Seth introduced his two co-workers, Sheila and Tammy, and said I had five minutes to tell them about the Go! Go! Sports Girls. I took a deep breath and gave them my best possible five-minute pitch. They studied the dolls quietly as I anxiously awaited their response.

"I would love to put your dolls on Walmart.com," Seth answered after what felt like an eternity.

"They're already on Walmart.com," I responded, trying not to seem disappointed.

Then Sheila spoke up. She was older than Seth, quiet and confident. She appeared to be in a position higher than Seth, but I wasn't sure. She pointed to sample packaging I had created to display Soccer Girl Cassie's story and doll, and asked, "What is that?"

I handed over the display, and she started reading the book. I explained how I was considering launching a doll and book set.

"This is great," she said. "If you can write five more books to go along with the dolls and package them together, we'll put them in Walmart stores."

I had to make sure I heard her correctly, so repeated, "In addition to Soccer Girl, if I write five more books to go along with five different dolls, you'll put them in Walmart stores?" The words coming out of my mouth sounded too good to be true.

"Yes," she said, "Seth will get you set up as a vendor and be in contact with you next week." Unable to contain my excitement, I celebrated by thanking and hugging them all. I knew then that this was another small moment that was going to have a big impact.

The cell service at the Javits Center is terrible, so I went to the front of the building to call Kara. At this point she had drafts for three manuscripts. Not only would she be excited to hear the news, but she would also want as much time as she could to get writing the next three books. Before placing the call to Kara, I saw a slew of texts. They were from friends and family who saw me on *Fox & Friends*. I opened the first one from Roxanne: "Hi Dolly, (her nickname for me since college) Great interview this morning! You had some big hair going on, and what's with all the makeup?"

I hadn't seen myself since the segment and ran into the nearest bathroom. I looked at myself and started laughing. I just pitched to Walmart buyers looking like Lovely Lola! The irony. I patted down my hair and wiped some of the color off my face before going back out to make my call.

When Kara didn't pick up, I left her a message: "Kara! You're never going to believe what just happened! Walmart wants to put six doll and book sets in Walmart stores. You have to start writing more books! Call me!"

CHAPTER 21

READ & PLAYS COME TO LIFE

"Just when the caterpillar thought
the world was over, it became a butterfly."
— *Proverb*

When Kara called me back, she was equally over-whelmed and excited about the Walmart proposition. It was happening. We were challenging the status quo, and Walmart, the largest retailer in the world, just took notice.

This small moment got the ball rolling with a little more speed. As usual, I was in unchartered territory. When I founded Dream Big Toy Company and created the Go! Go! Sports Girls dolls, I knew nothing about the toy industry; now I was about to enter the publishing industry and work with the world's largest retailer. Up to this point I had learned the industry as I went along. If I had any familiarity or experience with anything it was figuring out what I didn't know.

Kara was a great publishing resource since she had written multiple published books. She taught me about the page I never paid attention to in a book, the copyright page. To this day, I never overlook this page in any book because it shares important information such as the author's dedication, the year the book was published, the publisher, copyrights, trademark, special legal instructions like "Permission is never granted for commercial purposes," and the library of congress control number.

In addition to the books and dolls selling at Walmart stores and Walmart.com, Kara and I wanted the books to be sold individually, separate from the dolls. We had visions of the Go! Go! Sports Girls books in large and independent bookstores, libraries, elementary schools, Amazon, and more. We were dreaming big, but why not? We were on a roll.

I began contacting large publishers with little or no response. We looked into custom publishers, small publishers, and self-publishers. Kara suggested we also reach out to distributers, which is when we connected with Independent Publishers Group (IPG), an independent book sales and distribution company in Chicago. On June 11, 2013, I sent a note through their online submission form and quickly received a response. They were interested! They loved the idea of lead female sports characters and explained they would sell the book throughout the world. On July 25, I signed the contract and began my publishing journey with the amazing, kind, and loyal IPG team.

Kara had completed books for Soccer Girl Cassie, Swimmer Girl Suzi, and Gymnastics Girl Maya, and we decided she would write books for the next three dolls that were selling well—Dancer Girl M.C. and Runner Girl Ella, but the next one was more difficult. Basketball Girl Kate and Cheerleader Girl Roxy were selling about the same. Both were not selling strongly, but Cheerleader

Girl seemed to be taking off in the southern states, so we agreed that would be our sixth book.

We also had to come up with a name for the doll and book set quickly because Walmart was putting pressure on me, and "Go! Go! Sports Girls Doll and Book Set" wasn't exactly catchy. We thought about it for days but didn't come up with anything we liked. Then one morning Kara called and said, "I've got it." (Over the years, I have witnessed and admired Kara's many "I've got it" moments when her lightbulb goes on. It's impressive!) She excitedly said, "The Go! Go! Sports Girls Read & Play!" She was right, and it stuck.

I needed an illustrator and editor, so I did what I did when creating the dolls: I asked a lot of questions. I interviewed a few people, but two women I interviewed I instantly had a good feeling about. Like Ina's feeling about me, I knew they were the ones. Pamela (Pam) Seatter, a talented art director who had worked on children's books with Disney, *Sesame Street*, Eric Carle, and more, became the Go! Go! Sports Girls illustrator. Susan (Susie) Rich Brooke, a seasoned editorial director became the series editor, and I can't think of a smarter and more talented team to create books with female lead characters that encouraged all kids to dream big and go for it. They were just as passionate as Kara and me.

We were eager to get to work. Kara took each doll and created a story that allowed her to learn about the sport and navigate social-emotional growth through that sport, whether self-confidence, courage, teamwork, or belonging. What Kara and I both understood as athletes is that sport is a conduit for personal growth. We wanted that reflected in the stories.

The social-emotional growth aspect to the books was important for the age we were trying to reach — as was the non-fiction component of the books that covered everything from the history of the sport, equipment required, and rules of the game. Staying true to the mission of Go! Go! Sports Girls, at the end of each book was a list of tips for how each character strived to be healthy. We intended these books to be early readers as opposed to picture books and set out on the process to find a company that could "level" the books to the appropriate reading level. Again, this was always one of those details I took for granted as my own three children learned to read.

While Kara, Susie, and Pam were busy creating, I was busy working with the Walmart team. First, I needed to get set up as a supplier in their online Retail Link system. This was not easy, and it took months. It felt like I was taking a crash course in a foreign language.

I'm far from being a computer whiz, but I forced myself to learn Walmart's Retail Link system. I would work on it for hours a day and late into the evenings, figuring out one step only to be perplexed by the next step. And there were no skipping steps. Each one had to be completed in order, and it felt like there were a thousand steps. Fortunately, Walmart offers a Retail Link hotline, which I sometimes called multiple times a day. I called so often I started recognizing voices of the person on the other end before they said their name. I'm sure they recognized mine too, and I bet they weren't too excited to hear my voice! There were some points during the setup process where I became so frustrated that all I wanted to do was put my head on my desk and cry, but I never did. Tears would not get Go! Go! Sports Girls on the shelves at Walmart.

With a new product, Walmart often does a test in a few stores to see how it performs. Seth wanted to do this with the Read & Plays and gave me a thirty-day test period in the spring of 2014. This was tight because we needed to have the six books completed, published, packaged with the dolls, shipped from China and at Walmart warehouses throughout the country by January. We had less than a year to pull it together, and I knew this was possible, but I wasn't confident. One thing I wouldn't allow was the pressure of the deadline to compromise the quality of the dolls, books, or brand.

With Pam's help, I worked on the package design. I went to many Walmart stores with my tape measurer in hand to study their toy aisles, see what caught my eye, and measure their store shelves. Every inch of Walmart shelves is worth money, so I had to make the packaging as small and appealing as possible. Like Target, Toys R Us, and every toy store, the girl toy aisle was a sea of pink with a splash of purple. I always knew the Read & Play packaging would not be pink or purple because my goal was to disrupt the pink aisle. My son Peter suggested blue, which is associated with feelings of freedom, intuition, imagination, inspiration, and sensitivity. It had to be a shade of blue.

I enjoyed working with Seth. He was very responsive, supportive, and patient with my novice questions, but in June he announced he was offered a promotion within

Walmart, and he would be leaving the toy department. I was sorry and nervous to see him go. The "what ifs" started racing through my mind. *What if the new buyer doesn't like my product as much as Seth? What if they decide to cancel my order? What if I end up with Walmart like I did with Target?*

I quickly learned that is not how Walmart works. Haley Kochen was the new girl toy buyer, and she was equally as great as Seth, taking over where he left off. It was a smooth transition. She invited me to their headquarters in Bentonville, Arkansas during their semi-annual vendor meeting event in October, so we could meet. It was like Target's vendor's meeting, except in a hard-to-get-to location.

I was thrilled because this is a coveted invitation. Not everyone gets invited to their headquarters, but it comes with a steep price. The airlines increase their airfare to Bentonville during Walmart's vendor meetings, so I paid close to $1,000 to fly for one hour and fifteen minutes from Chicago on a tiny little plane to a tiny little airport in Arkansas.

I arrived in Bentonville the morning of October 10, and it felt like a hot summer day. While Target's headquarters resemble a hip college campus, Walmart's headquarters look more like a Walmart store with no frills. The waiting room was small and filled with people I could tell were experienced with selling to Walmart. There were signs posted giving vendors directions on how to sign in through their computer system, and I nervously followed them thinking, *"what if"* this doesn't go through, and I miss my meeting? That very moment was when the fire alarm went off. I had the same feeling when I was bumped by the pope. Really? Today when I have my meeting?!

Thousands of people exited the building. Walmart's headquarters is very unassuming and sprawling. I was one of the first people to exit, so to see the thousands of people stream out of the building was like watching fifteen clowns climb out of a miniature car. Where were all these people coming from? We were sent to stand in the parking lots while fire trucks and police cars surrounded the building.

People were still on edge from the Boston Marathon bombing in April, and I could hear some speculate that it may be a terrorist threat or an actual fire. We stood on the black pavement sweltering in the heat for thirty minutes when we were given the all clear and told it was just a drill, and we could re-enter the building.

No one knew what to do. Vendors were looking for their buyers and buyers were looking for their vendors. I had no idea who was meeting me in the lobby, so I stood in the middle of the room, pulled a Go! Go! Sports Girls doll out of my bag and waited, hoping the doll would draw attention to the person I was supposed to meet. I was the last one standing in the lobby, and I thought "what if" my last "what if" was happening when a woman turned the corner and called my name. She apologized for being late, but the fire drill put their team behind. Phew!

I followed Susan Dux through a series of hallways that led to rows of small conference rooms. We entered one of the rooms where Haley and Tammy Mores were waiting for us. All three women loved the Go! Go! Sports Girls and were eager to help make them a success. Like

Target, we only had thirty minutes to speak. We discussed packaging requirements and details. Walmart does not budge when it comes to details. It is either done correctly, or you don't move forward, and you are fined. It's probably why they are the world's largest retailer. But Haley wanted to stress the importance of following Walmart's directions correctly.

Then we got to the part I'm sure every Walmart vendor dislikes discussing: pricing. Haley said she would like to see the Read & Plays retail around $10.99. I knew Walmart wanted low prices, but there was no way I could retail the product for that price. I explained to her my costs, and we agreed that the Read & Plays would retail at $14.99. It was still a good deal for Walmart, and I was still making a miniscule profit, but my hope was to eventually have the Go! Go! Sports Girls Read & Plays in all 4,756 US Walmart stores.

At the end of the meeting, Susan told me about Walmart's Women's Economic Empowerment Initiative. She explained how Walmart started it in 2012 to empower women in business. Through this initiative their goal was to source $20 billion from women-owned US businesses and double their sourcing in international markets; support training for one-million women in product supply chains in skills relevant for career advancement and market access; and work to increase diversity and inclusion in their supply chain.[1]

She gave me a contact to call, and the following week I became part of their initiative. Most of Walmart's cus-

---

[1]   Walmart.com, Women's Economic Empowerment.

tomers are women, and they found that women are drawn to items that are from women-owned business, so by being part of this initiative, every product has a "Women Owned Business" seal on the front of the packaging. I was proud to display these important words.

Two days after meeting with Haley and her team, she emailed me my first Walmart order for 2,000 Read & Plays to be tested in fifty stores throughout the Midwest starting March 31. It was happening! And good thing, too, because doll manufacturing and book production was already underway to meet the time constraints.

Soon we would provide a much-needed choice in the toy AND book marketplace, one that was age-appropriate, represented the way girls really lived, and highlighted what a girl's body could do rather than what it looked like. Walmart was helping me fulfill my mission to push what's possible for girls throughout the US…and hopefully soon throughout the world.

CHAPTER 22

PERSEVERANCE PAYS OFF

"If you don't go after what you want,
you'll never have it. If you don't ask, the answer is
always no. If you don't step forward,
you're always in the same place."
— *Nora Roberts*

I didn't make the deadline. In January 2014, my factory informed me that the Read & Plays would not arrive in the states until April 5. I had to break the news to Haley, and my fear and "what if" worries kept me up at night. *What if she cancels the order? What if I was wrong to think I could figure out a way to deal with it?*

On January 8th, I sent Haley an email explaining my situation. I waited patiently and anxiously for her response. One day went by and no response, then the next, and next, then a week, until I officially began to freak out. My "what ifs" were happening! Eight days later I finally got an email from Haley that said, "Yes, we will make this work. We will move the test to June."

Phew. Again. I began to realize my "what ifs" were my own fears—my fear of failure and rejection, and I needed to outsmart my fears, because they were bubbling up too often. I was giving these negative hypotheticals too much energy—energy that was holding me back when I needed to use all of my energy to move forward. Regardless, harboring fear was not good for my mental, emotional, and physical health. From that moment on, I decided to step over my fears, believe in success, and dig deep to find courage, or at least try.

Between January and June, I added another prestigious award to my list: Creative Child Product of the Year Award. Not a top ten award but THE product of the year! I was honored. I was also asked to speak at my first speaking engagement on behalf of Walmart at the February toy fair "Women in Toys and Walmart Entrepreneurs Forum." It was my first speaking event, and during the event, Walmart introduced me as their posterchild. A strange choice of words, but I knew they were behind me and the Go! Go! Sports Girls 100 percent.

The test period was thirty days, and I was determined to make it a success, and I had a plan. The Read & Play packaging was blue and would sit on the shelves amid the sea of pink, but I wanted them to stand out even more because I was still competing with recognizable brands; My Little Pony Princess, Monster High Dolls, and of course Barbie to name a few. I asked Haley if I could have the endcaps in the fifty stores. An endcap is a display for a product placed at the end of an aisle that can give a brand a competitive advantage. Products on endcaps generally sell much faster than products not on endcaps, and it comes with a price tag to manufacturers. I knew it was a longshot because I could not afford to pay for the endcap, but I knew the importance of the ask.

Her response was YES, and this was huge.

I needed to make sure the Read & Plays sold. Through Walmart's Retail Link system, I was able to see the stores Haley assigned, and they were in Indiana, Illinois, and Wisconsin. This was fortunate because I had many family members and friends living in Indiana and Illinois, and Steve had family in Wisconsin. I reached out to everyone I knew and asked them to go to their local Walmart store and buy the Read & Plays to keep on hand for future birthday or holiday gifts. I also asked them to reach out to their friends and ask them to do the same. I was going about this the old-fashioned way by word of mouth, or like the 1980s Faberge Organics shampoo commercial: "And they'll tell two friends, and so on, and so on."

My next idea was different and another longshot. I asked Haley if Kara, Pam, and I could do book signings at Walmarts in Illinois. She paused then gave a little laugh and said, "I don't think Walmart stores have ever had a book signing, but I like the idea." She suggested I reach out to the individual store managers to make arrangements. Kara and I began calling stores immediately.

My experience working with Walmart's headquarters was very positive, and for the most part, I always received a quick response. This wasn't the same at the store level. There were no email addresses, so calling was the only option, and many of our calls were never answered or returned. It was time consuming and frustrating, but we secured book signings at six Walmarts over a two-day period.

Kara flew in from Minneapolis and met Pam and me at the stores, and we began our Walmart book signing tour. We made quite the entrance carrying a table, chairs, and the giant five-foot Soccer Girl Cassie doll, but it worked, and we sold the Read & Plays.

Each day I checked the Retail Link to see the number of Read & Plays sold at each store. Soccer Girl Cassie, Dancer Girl M.C., Swimmer Girl Suzi, and Gymnastic Girl Maya were doing great, but the other two, Runner Girl Ella and Cheerleader Girl Roxy, weren't selling as well. I also noticed some stores sold zero Read & Plays which concerned me. Kara and I began calling store managers again and learned that because the Read & Plays weren't a modular item (an item that is replenished like Barbie, Monster High, toothpaste, and shampoo), it would take time to find space on the shelves.

Frustrated, I drove to a few Walmarts in Illinois to speak to managers. At the first store I was told the manager was in the office, and he would meet me at the back of the store. I walked over and waited for what seemed like an eternity, but was probably only fifteen minutes. I was annoyed and wasn't about to let one person stand in the way of everything I had worked so hard for. I felt a wave of fearlessness come over me. Then I opened the door and let myself in.

The back room was stacked with boxes waiting to be unpacked. I knocked on a few office doors with no answer until I came to one with the manager in it. I explained my situation, but he was unsympathetic and dismissive. He asked me to wait again. I agreed, but I had a different plan. I began asking people working in the warehouse if they could help me find the Read & Plays by Dream Big Toy Company. They did and I loaded the Read & Plays onto a moving cart, rolled them to the toy aisle, and found space on the endcaps.

Driving to the next few stores, I knew what I had to do to get my product on the endcaps in the toy aisles, but this time I would bypass the managers and go directly into the back room. Talk about disrupting the pink aisle! I was determined to make this work and give girls an empowering option on toy store shelves—even if that meant stocking the shelves myself.

By the end of June, I wasn't sure if Haley would see the test as a success or a failure. There were still stores I could see showing zero sales, while other stores were selling out. On July 15, 2014, I had a fifteen-minute phone call scheduled with Haley. I was nervous because I had no idea what to expect, but I wouldn't allow the "what ifs" to take over. I knew I gave it my best shot, and if she didn't want to move forward, I had still learned a lot and enjoyed the experience.

She told me she had good news and to my surprise the test was successful. She would be placing the Go! Go! Sports Girls Read & Plays in 200 stores throughout the country starting in February 2015 but would only move forward with the top four selling Read & Plays: Soccer Girl Cassie, Dancer Girl M.C., Swimmer Girl Suzi, and Gymnastic Girl Maya.

I made it to the next level, and I was moving forward. As thrilled as I was, I knew all too well that new opportunities brought new obstacles. By now, I was familiar with the term "cautiously optimistic," and I was cautiously optimistic entering this new phase with Walmart.

CHAPTER 23

HIGHS AND LOWS

"If you're always trying to be normal,
you'll never know how amazing you can be."
– *Maya Angelou*

Soon after getting the good news from Walmart, I received an exciting email from Natalie Zmuda, Deputy Managing Editor with Ad Age. She wrote:

Hi Jodi –

I'm an editor with Advertising Age. I'm working on a story about the recent spate of ads seeking to empower women and girls from Always, Pantene and Verizon. As someone who has been immersed in this space for some time, I'd be curious to hear your perspective on these ads, which, of course, follow in the footsteps of Dove.

I'm interested in whether you've observed a shift in the market in the years since you launched your company. Are empowering messages for girls gaining wider notice and interest? If so, why do you think that is?

Would you be available for a few minutes sometime this week?

Thanks,
Natalie

I was flattered my doll brand was on the radar of a national business magazine. Ad Age, marketed as a "must-read for an influential audience of decision makers and disruptors across the marketing and media landscape,"[1] was taking notice, saw me as a disruptor, and considered my expertise valuable to their readers. Natalie went on to feature me in two Ad Age articles in September 2014, *Less Talk, More Women at the Top* and *Female Empowerment in Ads: Soft Feminism or Soft Soap?*

Momentum was building, and I wanted it to continue into the launch of the Read & Play sets. I knew I couldn't let up. I was still doing my own marketing and publicity, and now Kara was a willing sidekick to help brainstorm ideas, think through promotional tactics, and write pitches and social media posts. We decided it would be a good idea to get testimonials from accomplished and well-known moms, so we did what we were beginning to do very well: We asked. The result was some outstanding endorsements from some amazing moms:

> *"Swimming is part of my daughter's life too, so when she plays with the Go! Go! Sports Girl swimmer doll it's fun to watch as both a mom and athlete. I love the message the Go! Go! Sports Girls dolls and books promote, and glad my active daughter has something like this to identify with and to inspire her."* **Dara Torres, Twelve-Time Olympic Champion**

---

1   "Adage about Us | AD Age" (Advertising Age, n.d.), https://adage.com/help/about-us.

"Ruby and I absolutely love Ella! She is so cute and has such a great story to go with her. Being an Olympic runner and now a mommy, it is so important to me to help my children learn early on how to be active and stay healthy. Ella's story teaches us so much about running but more importantly it teaches goal setting and family fitness. I would recommend this for anyone and I can't wait to get more of the dolls and books for my nieces! Such a great way to teach all of us to continue to Get After It in life!" **Carrie Tollefson, 2004 Olympian, Athletics TV/ Web Analyst**

"Go! Go! Sports Girls founder, Jodi Bondi Norgaard, is creating true alternatives for girls. The Go! Go! Sports Girls books and dolls empower girls to be active, encourage creative play through sports and promote healthy life skills. My daughters and I love them!" **Jennifer Siebel Newsom, First Partner of California, Filmmaker of Miss Representation *and* The Mask You Live In**

"Growing up, my mom told me I could be anything I wanted to be with hard work and perseverance. The Go! Go! Sports Girls offer girls the same message. I highly recommend the dolls and books for kids who want good role models and to achieve goals." **Gretchen Carlson, Journalist, Advocate, Author**

On December 1, 2014, just two months before the Read & Plays were to hit Walmart stores, Haley announced she was moving to a new department within Walmart. The transition from Seth to Haley was fairly easy, so I assumed the transition to Haley's new replacement would be easy as well.

Lisa Bowman replaced Haley, and her first email to all her suppliers was an outline of her expectations and commitments. She was all business, and she had rules. Unfortunately, we got off to a rocky start.

On January 5, 2015, my factory notified me that there was a defect in the yarn used for the dolls' hair, and my product would be arriving in the States two weeks late. I sent Lisa an email right away to let her know. While Seth and Haley had been patient with my minor setbacks, Lisa was not. She replied to my email quickly, "This is a big problem." Less than twenty minutes later, she sent a second email tagged with a high importance red exclamation point: "Jodi—just tried to call you. Again, this is a huge issue."

Knowing I needed to get this over with before panic and nerves paralyzed me, I immediately called Lisa. She was angry and reiterated her rules, saying a product arriving two weeks late was unacceptable. I calmly listened and gave her no excuses. I told her it was my fault, and it would never happen again. By the end of the conversation, I felt like I should have been hurt or upset, but I wasn't. I think she appreciated how I handled her frustration, and I appreciated her frankness.

At the end of January, my importer was the next to send me bad news. My shipment that was already two weeks late due to yarn issues was now stuck on a boat in the Pacific Ocean due to labor strikes at US ports. What could I do? I was at the mercy of the west coast ports, but Lisa was not happy and let me know.

My product was again delayed and still not on Walmart shelves. I felt like I had this big break, and forces beyond my control were keeping me from giving this opportunity my best shot. I had been there before.

Prior to having kids, Steve talked me into getting a dog. Not just any dog, but a smart, high energy, and somewhat crazy Weimaraner we named Max. Max was the runt of the litter and he grew to be a strong ninety pounds.

Maxie, as we sometimes called him, was gentle and sweet and made me laugh and cry. He also added chaos and stress to my life. His energy level was crazy. I couldn't just walk Max; I had to run him, so I became a runner, going out on daily three- to five-mile runs. I give him credit for getting me into really good shape, which eventually led me to finishing multiple half marathons and a marathon.

Max was my buddy when I worked running Basket Expressions. When I sat at my desk, he would climb on my chair behind me, scooching me forward, put his head on my left shoulder and fall asleep. When I was creating baskets, he was nearby where he could see me. He seemed to be familiar with my routine and knew the freezers and the basement contained good things to eat.

One spring, I was preparing to fill a large order for a client who was hosting an event in Chicago. Along with the baked goods, they requested a box of Frango mints in each basket. Frango mints are famous mint choco-late squares that are a treasured Chicago tradition originally sold at the beloved and iconic Chicago-based store, Marshall Field's. My dad was at my house helping with the kids when UPS delivered four large boxes each containing twenty-four smaller boxes of Frango mints sealed in plastic. Each small box contained four Frango mints. I opened one large box to make sure all was intact, then placed the four large boxes on our kitchen table thinking they were safe and out of Max's reach. My dad and I left with the kids to have lunch. The dog successfully opened all twenty-four sealed boxes in one hour and ate ninety-six Frango mints. I rushed him to the veterinarian to get his stomach pumped. Twenty-four hours later, he was back to normal.

I was determined to be more careful. One day, after my baked goods were delivered, I put the box of cookies on top of my workspace against the wall where they seemed out of Max's reach. I should have known better. I left the house with the kids and returned to find Max eating the last of the fifty cookies. Again, I rushed him to the vet, had his stomach pumped, and twenty-four hours later, he was back to normal.

After the cookie-eating incident, I felt defeated. I could not outsmart my own dog. I came to a crossroad. I was losing control of my business; my inventory was being eaten. I had lost control of my dog and realistically, he should have died from the toxic amount of chocolate he ate. For eight weeks out of the year, I worked fifteen-hour days seven days a week and inevitably would be sick for the first two weeks of January.

I knew it was time to sell the business. I was fortunate to find a buyer quickly and sold Basket Expressions in February 1999. I'm sure I would have eventually come to sell, but Maxie's "encouragement" helped me take the next step and move on. The decision to sell Basket Expressions was hard, but my gut told me I was doing the right thing.

Now, here I was, feeling at a similar crossroads with Go! Go! Sports Girls. Yet even with all the setbacks I was experiencing, I didn't want to let it go—my instincts were telling me to stick with it, keep fighting, and have faith.

CHAPTER 24

STAYING ALIVE

"Keep a little fire burning; however small,
however hidden."
– *Cormac McCarthy*

The week after getting the news about my delayed shipment, Steve had a meeting in Phoenix, and I decided to join him. I needed a break. I felt like no matter how hard I worked, something got in my way. I didn't feel like working. I didn't feel I could take another setback. The weather didn't help either. February in Chicago is cold and dreary, so it was a welcome escape. The first morning in our hotel room, I told Steve about my frustration and concerns and that I was exhausted.

"Maybe now is the time to throw in the towel," he said. "We're both working hard, but you're barely bringing in any money. You're not being financially rewarded for all the effort you're putting in."

I hated hearing those words, but he was right. I worked hard and made very little money. Sure, I wanted to make money, but I was also creating change and fighting for something so important. There had to be value in that. I thought this but didn't say it. I knew I had to be realistic too. Maybe he was right, and it was time to throw in the towel.

Steve left our hotel room to attend his meeting, and I stayed in bed in my pajamas. I felt immobilized. I could hardly bear the thought of walking away from all I had worked toward. I stared at the ceiling and thought, *why can't I make this work? What could I have done differently?*

That's when my cell phone rang, jerking me out of my catatonic state. Even though I didn't want to talk to anyone, I slowly reached over to the bedside table. I held the phone up to my face, read the name, and popped out of bed. The caller ID said NBC.

NBC! My heart raced as I fumbled to hit the right button to answer. The person on the other end said, "Hi, Jodi, my name is Stephanie and I'm a producer with the *Today Show*. With Toy Fair coming up in a few weeks, we would like to do a feature on you and other women creating change in the toy industry."

I thought, *I'm alive! I'm not throwing in the towel!* The *Today Show* doesn't do features on just anyone! How could I give up now? Stephanie explained that a *Today Show* crew would come to Toy Fair to interview me, Bettina and Alice with Roominate, and Debbie with GoldieBlox. I called Christy and asked if I could share her booth with her for a day because I was going to Toy Fair one more time.

On February 14, 2015, I waited patiently and excitedly for the *Today Show* crew to arrive with one of their hosts, Erica Hill. Erica interviewed me first, then she and her crew walked to the Roominate booth to interview Alice and Bettina, then to the GoldieBlox booth to interview Debbie. We had to wait a week for the segment to air, but on February 22 at 9:11 a.m. it was on, and I was reinvigorated by the title: "Girls' toys? Group of women revolutionize the toy aisle: TODAY's Erica Hill talks with the powerful women behind the newest, innovative next generation of toys for girls."

I was alive.

CHAPTER 25

BE CAREFUL WHAT YOU WISH FOR

"My favorite thing about girl power is that over time
it turns into woman power."
– *Cleo Wade*

Word got out at Toy Fair that *The Today Show* was not interviewing Mattel, MGA Entertainment, or Ty but three *small* women-owned businesses who were shaking up the toy industry. There was also a fair amount of buzz because the Go! Go! Sports Girls Read & Play won another Oppenheim Toy Portfolio Platinum Award.

The attention was great, but now that my product was going in Walmart (as soon as it arrived), smaller and medium sized stores were hesitant to carry the dolls. As "specialty" stores, they wanted to distance themselves from what customers could find on the aisles of a big-box store, and it was difficult for them to compete with big-box prices. I knew I had all my eggs in one basket, but it was a big basket. I was at peace with that. And with Walmart behind me, people who wanted to help grow my business began to step forward.

At Toy Fair, I met Knute with Brybelly, an Amazon distributor located in southern Indiana, who I eventually hired to handle Amazon orders. I met Genji and Kristin with Product Greenhouse located in Chicago. I hired these sharp women as my new sourcing company. They helped not only with the manufacturing and shipping, but also with the doll and packaging design. They created a livelier face, designed new doll clothing, and added wire to the limbs so the dolls were now posable into whatever action a little girl imagined. Their input often bested my own ideas or offered new approaches I had never considered, which took my product to another level. I was grateful and glad I was the kind of entrepreneur who had an open mind toward the expertise of others.

I also met with Beth who owned Playrific and created educational apps for brands. She had a young daughter and loved the mission of Go! Go! Sports Girls. She asked if she could create apps for the brand.

"I love the idea, but I can't pay you," I told her, the same way I replied to Kara years ago.

"I'll do it at no charge," she responded, "Girls need to see positive images, and I want to be part of the project." She went on to create amazing online puzzles and games for the Go! Go! Sports Girls, extending my brand into the hands of children in a way young children have come to expect.

My licensing agents, Joan Packard Luks, Women in Toys president, and her partner David Wollos at The ThinkTank Emporium suggested it was time to pitch the Go! Go! Sports Girls to networks and consider licensing to extend the brand into different categories such as sporting goods, back to school, bedding, and so much more. I had significant interest, support, and momentum from so many directions.

This is the place in my story where I thought the dolls had real potential to take off and become a household brand. The kindness and support I was receiving—the excitement for the product and its mission—was at an all-time high. I thought this was the point in time when girls would finally have a choice in how they wanted to be represented by the dolls they played with, and the market would want nothing more than to provide that choice. But I wasn't at that point; I was still far from it.

The port strike ended at the end of February 2015. The Read & Plays finally arrived in the US, and by March they were on Walmart store shelves. I hired a warehouse in Illinois to store, fulfill, and ship my orders. I had a good system and followed all the Walmart rules. Every Sunday evening, I was excited to go into Retail Link to see the orders come in (and to use the system I had worked so hard to learn).

To keep the momentum going and boost my presence with specialty toy stores, I started working with Diverse Marketing, a large manufacturing rep group with a good reputation who had showrooms in Dallas and Atlanta. I believed I could win over specialty toy stores because the Read & Plays were only in 200 Walmart stores, and Diverse Marketing saw the potential.

Kara and I traveled to two gift markets that year, one in Atlanta in August and the other in Dallas in October. The gift markets are different from Toy Fair in that they are smaller shows focused on gifts as well as toys, and most of the rep groups have permanent showrooms in market centers where the shows are held.

At the Dallas show, we had the opportunity to meet with the Diverse sales team from all over the country to present the Go! Go! Sports Girls. The presentation to the forty salespeople was unusual. During the presentation, Kara and I had the feeling that 60 percent of the people were onboard and loved the Go! Go! Sports Girls, but the other 40 percent wanted nothing to do with the dolls and books. Afterward, one sales rep told me she thought the dolls were scary looking. I had other salespeople who would walk right past me and Kara without saying a word after we said hello. I had never had such a rude reception to the dolls before.

At the time it was confusing, and we felt snubbed. After more time observing the sales reps' reactions to other products, Kara and I noticed they tended to have an affinity for licensed toys from already popular characters. By contrast, the Go! Go! Sports Girls weren't a quick sell. They weren't a household name, thus requiring more energy and effort into the sales pitch. The Go! Go! Sports Girls didn't have their own show or movie, but they did have a story, which required someone willing to take the time to tell it. They weren't fashion dolls. No matter how hard we tried to incite enthusiasm for the dolls and books—that they were worth time invested with their buyers—it was hard to compete with bobbleheads that could sell themselves.

I think Kara was more annoyed than me because sadly I had become numb to the negative comments and rejection in the toy industry.

I still had one thing to look forward to while I was in Dallas: a meeting with Lisa, my Walmart toy buyer. If that sounds sarcastic after all that had happened between us, know I'm being sincere. By then my relationship with Lisa improved a lot. In fact, she became one of my favorite people to work with. I followed her rules. If I had a question, problem, or concern big or small, I communicated with her. She did not like any loose ends and/or surprises. Where some buyers would be annoyed with the constant emails and phone calls, she was patient and appreciative. Lisa had strong leadership skills that I admired. Sure, she was demanding, assertive, strong, decisive, and direct—behaviors in men that are highly regarded but far too often condemned in women. I liked her style and strength because she was also honest, smart, responsive, and supportive.

I finally had the opportunity to meet her in person after nine months of working with her. On the last day of the show, Kara was at a book signing, and I waited to meet with Lisa. I didn't know what to expect. She had a reputation of being a badass in the toy industry, which I had witnessed, and I was kind of afraid and nervous to meet her.

At our 4:00 p.m. meeting time, I saw Lisa approaching my booth with her team. She looked like she was on a mission, and I stood there as stiff as a board. When she saw me, she smiled, sat in the one chair that was close to me, and told me she was exhausted. I smiled back, and told her I was glad the one chair on the entire floor was next to my display. She laughed and as she rubbed her feet, said, "Jodi, can I tell you how much…"

My mind started filling in the words...*how much I dislike...how much time I've spent trying to work with you...how much I regret to tell you....*

Then she said, "...how much I love your product."

My heart skipped a beat, and my stomach did a back flip.

She went on to say, "Walmart isn't making much money off your product, but girls need to see better images, and the Go! Go! Sports Girls need to be on toy store shelves."

When I recently spoke with Anne Marie Kehoe, she explained that Walmart buyers have goals to improve diversity, and part of their performance review is the supplier diversity scorecard. While at Walmart, she encouraged and educated her buyers to work with small suppliers to help bring diversity and innovation to Walmart shelves. "And this is not easy because buyers have to be willing to see the benefits and break the paradigm," she said. "It's not a payoff for tomorrow. It's the potential for change in two or three years."

After spending most of the year in fear I would be dropped from Walmart, I was getting sincere validation for all the time and effort I had spent believing in this product. With Walmart's support I had a legitimate foothold in the toy market and reason to believe more retailers would come to see what Lisa saw in the product.

Thanks to a few personal connections, years later I sent Rob Walton, the son of Walmart founder Sam Walton and retired chairman of Walmart's board of directors, an email naming every person within Walmart who helped and supported me. I thanked him and Walmart for giving me a chance and being part of change. He responded:

Hi Jodi,

Thank you so much for sending your wonderful note. It is great to hear when we do something well. And, of course wonderful that you took advantage of the opportunity and ran with it! Congratulations.

I will pass your note on to some of our executives.

Best wishes,
Rob

I will always be grateful to Walmart for taking a chance on a small product, my product, for a potential big impact for cultural change.

CHAPTER 26

SOCIAL MEDIA SAVVY

"Make your own trail!"
— Katharine Hepburn

My main retailers were Walmart and Amazon. I still worked with Target.com, ToysRUs.com, and other .coms, but Walmart and Amazon kept me busy and in business. I was finally making money but still not taking a salary. I was thrilled to be in a position to pay Kara her royalties. My Walmart orders were increasing weekly, so I knew I would soon have to place another order with my factory.

Knute and Brybelly had done a great job setting up a Go! Go! Sports Girls store on Amazon, taking professional pictures of the dolls and books and using the right words to drive traffic to the site. And unlike Walmart, the Read & Plays for Cheerleader Girl Roxy and Runner Girl Ella were available for purchase.

I thought there was a good chance Walmart would expand the number of stores that offered Read & Play sets but figured I could increase those odds with more buzz around the product. As far as I had come, there still wasn't great awareness. I would feel more comfortable placing that next order with a bump in sales. I wanted to drive up demand but didn't have a lot of money to spend. I needed to be creative.

So far, my social media strategy consisted of Kara and I posting relevant product information to a Go! Go! Sports Girls Facebook and Twitter account, sharing information about female representation in the toy and book industry, and shouting out to others who were doing similar work. For about eight months, one of Kara's daughters posted to an Instagram account we created for Gymnastics Girl Maya (the top selling book). Maya's Instagram, with all of forty-seven followers, did not go viral, but we were doing what we could with the resources and time we had while also trying to keep the product alive and not completely ignore our families.

In order to create a more robust and efficient online presence, I contacted Genji and Kristen with Product Greenhouse to brainstorm with Kara and me, and we decided we would start with a focused social media campaign—something catchy, something worthy of sharing, something likeable. We knew there were plenty of people out there who identified with the message of girl empowerment, and if we could reach them, they could join our growing team of virtual fans. Virtual fans, we believed, would remember the Go! Go! Sports Girls when they needed that perfect birthday gift for their niece or daughter or best friend's kid.

While we knew what we wanted the campaign to do, we ended the meeting without knowing what that would look like. A few days later, Kara called one morning and said in typical Kara fashion, "I've got it! We can call the campaign 'Athlete is the New Princess,' with the tag line,

'Be Fierce and Sparkle.'" We started thinking about various words that fell on the athlete and princess continuum and clever ways to highlight the dichotomy. We discovered many homonyms that could make for a fun play on words. The most obvious being "ball," integral to most girls playing sports like soccer and tennis but also considered the pinnacle moment in a princess story.

Then we got to work on phrases and visuals for catchy memes that put in juxtaposition the stereotype of the princess with girls as they really are: strong, smart, and adventurous. We wanted something sharable that would make our point and resonate with the doll buyers of the world. In June 2015 I hired Wishpond, a company focused on social promotions to help us create those memes.

I posted a meme weekly and boosted its viewing by running a small but paid ad campaign on Twitter and Facebook for the entire week.

In addition to the memes, we wanted to engage more with our customers. At the beginning of each month, we asked parents to send us pictures of their sports girl being active and sporty, and at the end of the month we would randomly select a winner to receive a Go! Go! Sports Girls Read & Play.

At the start of the Athlete is the New Princess campaign, a friend of Kara's shared a Reebok campaign photograph of young girls around six years old dressed in blue princess dresses, wearing softball cleats and eye black, holding bats and mitts, and giving their fiercest look. This friend had a connection to Reebok, and Kara contacted them.

Hello Yujin,

My friend Darcy passed along your email to me —
you might remember her helping out the Reebok
shoot last weekend. Darcy is hard to forget even
when she isn't nine months pregnant!

I am the author of the Go! Go! Sports Girls book
series and I've copied Jodi Norgaard, owner of the
Go! Go! Sports Girl dolls. We both love what this
little girls' softball team has accomplished and I know
Jodi would like to send the members of the team their
own Go! Go! Sports Girls Dolls. Part of our message
(along with the company motto: Dream Big and Go
For It!) is that girls play sports and so should their
dolls. This team has put another spin on it: Girls play
sports and so should their princesses!

If you can help us facilitate sending them these
products, we'd very much appreciate it!

All best,
Kara

An hour later Kara received a response.

Hi Kara,

Amazing—the girls will love it! I've included
Betsy Gregory on the email—she is the photogra-
pher behind the genius photograph and also mom
to one of the girls.

Thanks!
Yujin

With Betsy's permission, I sent the girls Read & Plays, and Kara's "ask" lead to Betsy, Reebok, and Disney (they were part of the Reebok campaign) allowing me permission to use Betsy's fabulous and fierce photographs for the Go! Go! Sports Girls. This was the photograph that embodied our social media campaign.

The social media campaign, which continued for six months, was successful in adding more followers, but it didn't translate into the kind of awareness I needed to boost sales. However, I loved our innovation, creativity, and collaboration. The effort strengthened the brand with a relatable message, memorable professional photographs, and hundreds of heartwarming posts of fierce sporty girls showing off what their minds and bodies CAN do.

Sales were steady enough that I needed to place another larger order with my factory, yet I didn't have that definitive bump, which made capital an issue. At the beginning of 2016, I felt encouraged by how far I had come and at the same time disappointed that I couldn't generate enough sales to fund the next order. I was back to a position of should I or shouldn't I. Yet something always stirred my optimism. This time, it would be an invitation to the White House.

CHAPTER 27

INVITATION TO THE WHITE HOUSE

"We must carry forward the work of the women
who came before us and ensure our daughters
have no limits on their dreams, no obstacle to their
achievements, and no remaining ceilings to shatter."
– *Barack Obama*

The White House Council on Women and Girls

The U.S. Department of Education

&

*The Media, Diversity & Social Change Initiative
at the University of Southern California*

*Invite you to Participate in a Conference at the
White House Helping our Children Explore,
Learn, and Dream without Limits:*

Breaking Down Gender Stereotypes in Media and Toys

This is an email I received on February 18, 2016. It went on to say:

We know that children's interests, ambitions and skills can be shaped early on by the media they consume and the toys they play with—and this doesn't just affect their development, it affects the strength of our economy for decades to come.

STEM (Science, Technology, Engineering and Math) industries offer some of the highest-paying, most in-demand careers—there are over 600,000 unfilled jobs in information technology alone— yet, women hold only 28 percent of STEM jobs. And right now, communities across America are experiencing teacher shortages, and nursing is one of the fastest-growing professions—yet fewer than 25 percent of public-school teachers and only 9 percent of nurses are men.

How do we ensure that children's media and toys expose them to diverse role models and teach them a variety of skills so they can fulfill their potential and pursue their passions—and we as a nation can meet the needs of our workforce in the coming years?

We invite you to join representatives from toy, media, and retail companies; leaders of youth-serving organizations; researchers and scholars; educators; and others for a lively day of panels and presentations on breaking down gender stereotypes in children's media and toys. Renowned experts, innovators, and thought-leaders will be presenting current research, exciting case studies, and impactful new ideas to help all our children explore, learn, and dream without limits.

Date: Wednesday, April 6, 2016

Time: 8:30am–4:30pm

Location: Eisenhower Executive Office Building, South Court Auditorium, Washington, DC

RSVP: Please kindly reply by going to our RSVP Website and providing the requested information by Monday, February 29, 2016.

I was skeptical. *Did I just receive an invitation from the White House, or is it a scam?* I immediately called Kara to get her thoughts.

"You are not going to believe this email I just received," I said excitedly as I proceeded to read it to her. "Can this be for real?"

I still couldn't believe what I was reading. I kept repeating, "Is this for real?"

Kara was just as awestruck but had a little more faith in its authenticity. "Why not?" she asked back. "Why *not* you?"

There was a link attached for "RSVP Website,'" and I asked, "What do you think? Should I click on it? What if it's a scam, and my computer becomes filled with porn pictures?"

"Click it! You have to click it!" She said.

Nervously, I clicked it as Kara urged me on…and a screen popped up stating, "Welcome to the office of President Barak Obama."

No porn! It was for real! I was invited to the White House, and without hesitation, I responded YES.

The email came from Sarah Hurwitz, who I later learned was the senior speechwriter for President Barack Obama and head speechwriter for First Lady Michelle Obama. I was curious how they, the White House, heard about me, so I asked Sarah in an email. She replied, "You were suggested to us by one of our partners because of the Go! Go! Sports Girls. We'd love to have you!"

This was the ultimate validation to my hard work and mission, but Kara had worked hard on this mission too, and I wanted her to go with me. After asking Sarah if Kara could attend as well, she responded: "So unfortunately, space is very tight at this point—but I'd be happy to put Kara on a waitlist and let you know if spots open up. Would that work?"

On February 29, I received an email from Sarah: "It looks like there is room for Kara to come and I sent her an invitation." Kara and I were headed to the White House together!

The White House swore all the attendees to secrecy. We weren't allowed to do any promotions about the event or mention anything on social media. We had no idea who was attending, speaking at the event, or how large it would be, but I had a feeling my fellow change-makers in the toy industry would be there too.

One afternoon in March, I was speaking with Alice from Roominate, and at the end of the conversation I said inconspicuously, "Alice, will I see you in April?" She paused and slowly said, "Maybe? On the east coast?" I replied, "Yes!"

On April 5, Kara flew from Minneapolis to meet me in Chicago, and together we flew to Washington DC. As

Kara and I boarded the plane to take our seats in row 26, I saw a flight attendant who I knew. She was the mother of one of Peter's grade school classmates. I excitedly introduced her to Kara and briefly explained why we were headed to the White House. She said she was the attendant for first class but would come to the back of the plane to talk to us. An hour into the flight, she came to say hello with a platter of cheese, crackers, fruit, and two glasses of wine to celebrate. It was the prefect start to an amazing two days.

Prior to arriving to the White House, Kara and I were required to go through background checks, and the morning of the sixth, we were asked to arrive at the Eisenhower Executive Office Building an hour before the start of the 9:30 a.m. conference to give enough time to go through security. Anxious and excited, Kara and I woke up at the crack of dawn and headed to the conference by 7:30 a.m.

They were not exaggerating; it took an hour. There were multiple security screening checkpoints we had to go through staffed with military and dogs. It was a bit intimidating, but once we arrived at the South Court Auditorium, it was much more of a relaxed atmosphere.

As we entered the conference room, I saw Alice and Bettina from Roominate, Laurel from Wonder Crew, Julie from I am Elemental, and Debbie from Goldieblox. We were all invited. The six women disrupting the toy industry.

Kara and I had a plan. We had thirty minutes until the conference started, and we would divide up to meet as many people as possible. She didn't seem as nervous as I did and immediately started talking to a group of individuals. I needed to shake my nerves and study the surroundings. It was a small group of roughly 150 people. I was impressed we were invited, but I was feeling the imposter syndrome, "feelings of inadequacy despite evident success."[1]

I found two seats, put my things down, and had a quick self-pep talk. I thought, *get over yourself. Not everyone gets invited to the White House. You may never have this opportunity again. Kara is doing a great job. You can do it.* I stepped over my fear and introduced myself to a woman sitting alone.

She said her name was Diana Williams, and she was with Lucasfilm.

"As in *Star Wars*?" I said in awe. I had just gotten up the nerve to talk to someone, and the first person I meet works on the *Star Wars* franchise?

She nodded and went on to explain how she was part of the team that developed the 2015 *Star Wars: The Force Awakens*. I was so impressed and excited, and I wanted to know more. There was one thing in particular I wanted to know. I sat down next to her and asked, "What did you think about Hasbro merchandise not including Rey?"

After the film was released in December 2015, *Star Wars* fans began to notice that much of the merchandise didn't include Rey—who is obviously the main character and happens to be female. Hasbro owned the rights to produce licensed *Star Wars* toy merchandise, and people were angry with Hasbro about not including Rey, which reeked suspiciously of sexism. There was a huge

---

1   Gill Corkindale, "Overcoming Impostor Syndrome" (Harvard Business Review, April 6, 2023), https://hbr.org/2008/05/overcoming-impostor-syndrome.

#WheresRey social media campaign. Hasbro's explana-
tion was weak, stating: "Rey was not included to avoid
revealing a key plot line that she takes on Kylo Ren
and joins the Rebel Alliance."[2] People didn't buy their
excuse, and this wasn't the first time Hasbro has had this
kind of controversy. They excluded the female characters
Black Widow and Gamora from *Avengers* and *Guardians of
the Galaxy* action figure box sets, causing fan outrage.

Diana's response was shockingly good.

"When I found out about the omission of Rey," she
said with emotion and fire in her eyes, "I picked up the
phone and called the president of Hasbro and said, 'What
the fuck were you thinking?'"

I liked her! And I was instantly comfortable
in the room.

Rey was eventually added to the *Force Awakens* tie-in
merchandise, and I have to believe Diana was an instrumental force.

There were plenty of small toy companies in the room
willing to stand up and speak out against the powerful toy
and media status quo, to raise the standard for toys to better represent women and girls, but I was happy to see that
people like Diana, at a behemoth operation, was holding
the industry accountable too.

What was also running through the back of my
head was how I could have so much confidence in gen-
der-breaking dolls but a company like Hasbro, who could

---

2   Caroline Framke, "#WheresRey and the Big Star Wars Toy Con-
     troversy, Explained" (Vox, January 7, 2016), https://www.vox.
     com/2016/1/7/10726296/wheres-rey-star-wars-monopoly.

sell anything, chose not to produce a female doll for one of most powerful and lucrative franchises.

It comes down to numbers, according to friend and former vice president of marketing at the Miami-based toy company Jazwares, Karen Kilpatrick. "Past data is used for the present in toys and publishing. Everything is dictated by the past—past numbers, what has worked in the past, even when people and consumers want it to be different. Buyers are judged by a metric system. For something that doesn't have a track record or is new to the market, it takes time and it's a risk."

When buyers see something that works, then they will do it," she continued, adding that there are certain things buyers know that sell, for example fashion dolls and male action figures. "They fit into a category, a box. There are always certain boxes you have to fit into." And Rey didn't fit into that box.

At 9:30 a.m., we were asked to take our seats. The ground-breaking conference was about to begin. Sarah Hurwitz opened the conference, followed by Valerie Jarrett, Senior Advisor and Assistant to the President for Public Engagement and Intergovernmental Affairs, and chair of the White House Council on Women and Girls. For the next seven hours, we heard from educators, researchers, retailers, and media members on how to meet the challenge of breaking down gender stereotypes in media and toys.

There was great discussion on the need to close the gender gaps in our workforce by exposing children to diverse role models. Dr. Elizabeth Sweet, assistant professor at San Jose State University, shared findings from studies that reveal how toys are more divided by gender now than they were fifty years ago. By exposing children to toys, media, and role models beyond gender stereotypes, we offer them the opportunity to develop their talents and pursue their passions without limits, and as a nation we can meet the needs of our economy in the coming years.

Tina Tchen, Assistant to the President and Executive Director of the White House Council on Women and Girls, made the closing remarks. It was an amazing and informative day that Kara and I were proud to be a part of. Before leaving, I handed Tina a gift bag with dolls and books and a note for First Lady Michelle Obama, whose platform during her tenure as FLOTUS was Let's Move, an initiative to raise a healthier generation of kids.

Weeks later, I received in the mail a letter from the White House.

Dear Jodi and Kara:

Thank you so much for the generous gifts. It was such a nice gesture, and I hope you know how much I appreciate your thoughtfulness.

The support of people all over the country continues to amaze me, and I am filled with a great sense of hope for our shared future. Again, thank you for your kindness. I wish you all the best.

Sincerely,
Michelle Obama

Sadly, the Trump administration disbanded the Council on Women and Girls. But that day, it was validating to be recognized as a leader by the White House. The high-profile relationships and resources I made speak to the value that administration placed on women and girls, and the urgency needed to speed up the dreadful 130 years predicted by the World Economic Forum to reach gender equality. It was a career-defining moment, but I wasn't sure it would save my company.

PART 4

This Fight Is Still Not Over

CHAPTER 28

A TOY IS NOT JUST A TOY

"There is always light, if only we're brave enough to
see it. If only we're brave enough to be it."
— *Amanda Gorman*

I walked away from the conference feeling like I wasn't
some crazy lady making a stink about crappy choices
on the toy shelves. I had confirmation that there is a lot
wrong with the toy and media industries, and the office
of President Obama validated my effort and all the small
companies out there working hard to make a difference.

When President Obama established the White House
Council on Women and Girls in 2009, his administration
championed a number of gender equality issues, including equal pay, more science and technology education,
and laws for sexual assault. And they used their power to
draw attention to the stereotypes in toys.

Assistant to the President and Executive Director
of the White House Council on Women and Girls, Tina
Tchen stated, "I've been shopping in toy stores for 25
years and didn't realize what was happening. I was being
directed to the boys 7–12 section or the girls 7–12 section
of the toy stores, and that right there directs you to very
specific toys, divided by gender."[1]

---

1   Gregory Korte, "New Frontier for White House Women and Girls
     Initiative: Toys" (USA Today, April 6, 2016), https://www.usatoday.
     com/story/news/politics/2016/04/06/new-frontier-white-house-wom-
     en-and-girls-initiative-toys/82689976/.

Prior to the meeting, the White House received commitments for change from a number of large toy and media companies:

- *Family Fun* and *Parents* magazines will consider whether toys perpetuate gender stereotypes when they review new toys.

- Discovery Communications will launch initiatives to promote gender equality and highlight STEM skills.

- Girls Inc. and Girl Scouts will work to raise awareness about gender stereotypes in the media.

- *TIME for Kids* magazine will focus on stories about people, programs, or initiatives that break gender barriers.

- Netflix will renew *Project Mc²* which features four science-skilled girls recruited as spies.

Just getting this on the radar of toy and media companies was an important first step. To have them consider next steps and put them in writing? Smelled like progress to me! The companies were true to their word. They did implement these commitments.

But here's the catch: sometimes toy company executives have a strange interpretation of "breaking gender stereotypes," or at least bend that interpretation into familiar products with a proven track record.

Take, for instance, the problem with *Project Mc²*, an original Netflix series about four super-smart teenage girls who use their science and tech skills to save the day that premiered in 2015. While the show's goal was to inspire girls to unlock their own STEM potential, their licensing company, MGA Entertainment (the world's largest private toy company and maker of Bratz dolls), fell short on the challenge.

MGA Entertainment CEO, Isaac Larian, said in a press release, Aug 7, 2015: "My goal with the Project Mc² franchise is to encourage girls everywhere to be interested and pursue S.T.E.A.M-based careers, so in my lifetime, I can see the CEO of Apple, Amazon or Intel be a woman. It is a dream come true for MGA to bring this entertainment franchise to life in order to empower young girls to learn, play and explore the world around them on all of the platforms where they are engaged; from retail, to TV and online."

Sounds good, right?

But here's what Larian and his team approved for MGA's products in the *Project Mc²* line:

- "*Project Mc²* Color Change Makeup Kit to create the perfect look for saving the world. Pretty brilliant!"

- "*Project Mc²* UV Nail Maker. Use your cosmetic chemistry skills to design and make your own press-on nails and show off your unique style!"

- "Slumber Party Science Kit. After a mission, every undercover agent needs to rest and relax. These five awesome experiments let you make cucumber goggles, a rainbow face mask, facial scrub and more using household items."

If that isn't pigeonholing our girls, I don't know what is. It is an incredibly limited idea of encouraging STEAM (science, technology, engineering, art, and math) for young girls. I wish the head of Netflix had the guts of Diana from Lucasfilm to call Larian and say, "What the fuck were you thinking?"

By now, I hope I have pointed out enough patterns. The toy industry consistently pushes stereotypes that emphasizes what a girl should look like. Sure, you can be a spy and have interest in STEAM, but you better look pretty while doing it, which in turn also emphasizes how a girl should act. Our patriarchal culture continues to perpetuate gender roles by emphasizing the submissiveness and sexuality of women and girls.

This is precisely part of the problem discussed at length during the conference. Jess Weiner, cultural expert, and host of *The Smart Girl's Podcast*, stated, "six out of 10 girls won't do what they want because of the way they start feeling about themselves." And Rachel Simmons, parenting expert and *NYT* bestselling author stated, "We are asking girls for effortless perfection."

Toy companies are limiting our girls, not empowering them. Sure, there are other science kits on the market, but when a product is associated with a highly visible, highly promoted TV show, the product becomes more recognizable, which makes it an easy sell, and thus more profitable.

Big toy companies get a lot of credit for doing very little with minimal risk. In fact, one of the afternoon sessions at the White House conference was a panel consisting of representatives from Mattel, Disney, LEGO and DC Entertainment. Many small toy companies and academics were not happy they were considered the experts on breaking down gender stereotypes because their failure to address the issue is why many of us had started our companies in the first place—to *actually* break stereotypes.

One reason creating change is so hard is because still too few people see the harm. Make your own press-on nails—what's the big deal? The prevailing attitude of "it's just a toy" minimizes not only the profound effects and implications toys have on the growth and development of our children but also the sexualization and/or stereotyping itself. "It's no big deal" can apply as easily to a makeup kit packaged as a science kit to an unwanted sexual advance during a job interview.

Let's just stay with the idea that toys are more than child's play—that toys are more than a way for children to pass the time. Toys unlock creative ways of thinking, imagining the here and now, the future, and how children see themselves. Yes, rules, policies, and laws are vital to ensure equality, but they don't necessarily change mindsets. Minds are set in childhood. Toys matter.

Former president of Just Play, Sujata Luther, summed it up perfectly, "Toy companies are giving our kids what I call a 'Packaged Childhood.' They are packaging gender roles for kids from the time they are one year old. When we are introducing toys, we are not introducing our little kids to equality, our little girls to all sorts of role models. What we are putting in front of little girls and what we are saying is, you really should be a princess. Many companies don't change because it doesn't make sense to them monetarily and they are tapping into something that is so ingrained, not only in our children, but parents as well. Toy companies are packaging gender roles."

As parents we need to give as much consideration to the toys we put in our children's hands as we do the food in their mouths, the products on their skin, the media they consume, and other "ingestible things."

To a certain extent we trust the toys on the market as "safe," due to stringent testing and product safety guidelines, but even that is often trial by error.

I grew up in the '70s, and while there were some great toys, we now know they were downright dangerous. I loved Super Elastic Bubble Plastic, where you would squeeze a little bit of liquid plastic out of a tube, roll it into a ball, and blow it through a straw. My sister and I had hours of fun creating cool and colorful durable bubbles while feeling a calming lightheadedness. We were seven and ten years old, and we were getting high on plastic! It turns out the bubbles contained chemicals found in glue and nail polish remover.

Jarts was a family favorite. Played in two teams, we would throw lawn darts with metal spikes designed to fly in the air toward hula hoop sized circles where the other team was standing. It was a recipe for disaster. Overall, 6,100 people went to the emergency room because of the lawn darts.

The Water Wiggle was a summertime favorite. Similar to a sprinkler, but the toy, once fueled by the pressure of the water, would take off into the air flying and whipping in every direction, sparing no one from its wrath.

There have been other products and fads that have come before us that steered consumers into dangerous territory. "Junk food, now fortified with vitamins and minerals." "Cigarettes: Just what the doctor ordered." "Dieting? Try sugar."[2]

Seems ridiculous now, doesn't it? Sometime in the future will the masses think just as incredulously at, "*Project Mc2* Color Change Makeup Kit to create the perfect look for saving the world. Pretty brilliant!"

It's a no-brainer to pull toys from shelves that pose a physical risk of danger to children. So now ask yourself, would you buy your children a toy or let them watch a show that could damage their self-confidence and self-esteem and potentially prevent them from doing what they enjoy—a product that tells your strong, smart, and adventurous girl that it's not what her mind and body can do that's important, but what her body looks like? My guess is your answer, like mine, is no.

We don't have the same stringent consumer protections on our children's emotional and mental health as we do their physical health. And clearly large toy companies aren't making that a priority either.

"Any change has to be driven by a change in consumer attitudes," Tchen said during the conference. "We know by definition that companies are not non-profits. They're driven by consumer demand. Everyone has a role to play, including media and toy companies."

Debbie Sterling of Goldiblocks brilliantly points out a theory on why the toy industry is stuck in their ways. "At companies like Disney, Mattel, and Dream Works,

2   Hunter Oatman-Stanford, "What Were We Thinking? The Top 10 Most Dangerous Ads" (Collectors Weekly, August 22, 2012), https://www.collectorsweekly.com/articles/the-top-10-most-dangerous-ads/.

they have access to very expensive research and reports that have been done around kid play patterns. They look at these and think, 'Okay, the boy play patterns are construction toys and action figures. And the girl play patterns are nurturing and fashion.' These reports inform how toy and entertainment companies think about and design toys and media for children. But social media platforms like YouTube and TikTok have shown these reports are kind of bogus. When toys and media that break the rules of big toy and entertainment companies go viral, the big companies then think, 'Oh, well, wait a minute. Girls aren't supposed to like building, so what's going on here?'

There are deeply rooted beliefs about the way kids play that are held on to and they've been disproven again and again. The toy industry is really dominated, and has been for a long time, by a very small number of players, who wash, rinse, and repeat the same formulas for success that they've seen and they're generally pretty risk averse. Those are the players who give the feedback—girls only want fashion or girls don't like building. They follow their same formula, and don't innovate."

For far too long we have overlooked the gravity of influence the toy industry has on our children. But today's toys have become far too sexualized and gendered to be innocent playthings.

In the days and weeks after the conference, I felt more confident than ever in my mission. I believed a reckoning in the toy industry was long overdue.

CHAPTER 29

GAME CHANGING PHONE CALL

"A woman with a voice is, by definition,
a strong woman."
– *Melinda Gates*

I met Doyin Richards, a writer for the website Upworthy, at the White House. The following week he asked if he could include my story in an article about women creating change in the toy industry and asked for additional names. I agreed and gave him the names of the five women creating change: Laurel, Debbie, Julie, Bettina, and Alice. A few days later he contacted me and said his editor would like at least ten to twelve names of people changing the toy industry.

"Nope," I said firmly, "there aren't any more. It's just us, and we're working hard."

He wasn't sure his editor would allow him to move forward with the article, but the next day, Doyin contacted me and said the article was a go.

Doyin wrote, "Being told that girls are weak and soft and that boys are aggressive and unemotional is about as played out as the Macarena and Harlem Shake. Yet, it still happens often in our society. Here's the story behind cool toy companies you may not have heard of that are shattering stereotypes and helping kids believe they can be anything they want to be."[1]

With publicity from attending the White House conference and sales of the Read & Play at Walmart, I was busier than ever. This meant I was at my next crossroads. I needed workforce and capital. I had good options to explore; I could find investors, take out a loan from a bank, license the brand to a toy company, or sell it.

I researched investors and felt uneasy with that route. I saw the pressure and demands Debbie, Alice, and Bettina faced with their investors, and I was looking to get rid of pressure. A loan from the bank was too risky since Steve and I had self-funded the business, and we didn't want to invest anymore. Licensing or selling seemed like great options, but it's not easy. There are a lot more sellers than there are buyers.

But selling or licensing was the path I preferred, and I started reaching out to companies. Some I already had contacts with others were cold calls: Mattel, Hasbro, Spin Master, Jakks Pacific to name a few, but with no success.

I shared my capital dilemma with Karen Kilpatrick, who at the time was the Vice President of Marketing with Jazwares. She called me one afternoon in June.

"Our CEO and EVP have encouraged management to bring to their attention products we strongly believe

---

1   Doyin Richards, "Meet 4 Moms Who Created the One Toy They Wish They Had as Kids." (Upworthy, December 17, 2021), https://www.upworthy.com/meet-4-moms-who-created-the-one-toy-they-wish-they-had-as-kids.

in," Karen said. "I strongly believe in your brand. Can I present it to them?"

"Sure! When?"

"Right now," she said. "I'm going to meet with them now and will call you back."

I was shocked it was happening so quickly but also thrilled. I thought I would spend the next hour or so waiting for a response, but she called back five minutes later. Way too fast, I thought. I felt like I was receiving the dreaded thin envelope containing a rejection letter. I picked up the phone and in a somber voice said, "Hey."

I could feel the excitement in Karen's voice, "Well, that was easy! They want to acquire your brand!"

I was stunned. After ten years of fighting for girls and breaking gender stereotypes in media and toys, I was finally getting the opportunity I needed to move forward. I finally found a company who believed in my mission and brand. A company who was willing to take a chance and go outside the toy industry norm. I was finally going to have a team to help grow the Go! Go! Sports Girls, invest capital, and inspire and empower girls throughout the world. All that from an uninitiated phone call and an impromptu meeting.

Here was my third small moment that had a big impact on my entrepreneurial journey. It took five minutes with the US Open, five minutes with Walmart, five minutes with Jazwares, and about 2.5 million minutes in between.

We spent the next few months finalizing the contract, and by August, we agreed on a price. I would have a 5 percent interest in the brand, stay on as a consultant, have creative input, and become a public speaker to help with awareness of the brand and mission. I felt like I was staying involved enough while handing over the pieces—like manufacturing and distribution—I wanted to let go of. It wasn't exactly perfect, and I would have liked more money upfront, but I was on the lookout for a partner that could take Go! Go! Sports Girls to the next level, and I was ready to take a deal. I had been trying hard for some time to get the attention of big and small toy companies and was always hearing, "Your dolls are wonderful. We will discuss with our team." Then weeks later receiving a rejection email stating, "This product line is not a perfect fit for our company at this time." I felt companies were initially excited about the dolls, but then reality set in. The Go! Go! Sports Girls challenged the status quo and were not mainstream. They weren't fashion dolls. They would take work and were not an easy sell. But now, with Karen as my ally, I had confidence in this relationship. Jazwares was passionate about the mission, and everyone was excited to move forward.

In September 2016, Jazwares flew me to Miami to give a presentation on the Go! Go! Sports Girls. The morning of September 29, I met with the new Go! Go! Sports Girls/Jazwares team. There were about ten people who would help with design, branding, marketing, sales, content, and what's more, they seemed to share my desire to make the Go! Go! Sports Girls a household name. Ultimately, regardless of whatever financial outcome I received in return for the intellectual property, I wanted this brand to fulfill its mission and expand the choices available to girls.

After my presentation, I noticed a young woman with tears in her eyes.

"Is everything okay?" I asked.

"Thank you for doing this for every little girl," she said, wiping the tears from her face, "I played sports growing up, and I wish this would have been around when I was younger."

That meeting solidified the trust I had in Jazwares to carry on with everything I had worked so hard for. Their president and CCO Laura Zebersky was an athlete, a strong leader, and knew the importance of empowering girls. Maybe there hadn't been a bidding war for my brand, but I left Miami confident that Jazwares would take the Go! Go! Sports Girls to the next level.

For the next three months, I worked with my friend and speaking coach Brenda to help develop presentations to launch a speaking platform. My friends Joie and Jen, who own a web designing business, created a website and logo for me, and Kara helped me with the copy. Jazwares asked me to manage the Go! Go! Sports Girls social media, which I was happy to do.

2016 had been a great year. I was named one of twenty women who are changing the sport of running (and the world) by *Women's Running Magazine*, featuring the Read & Play for Running Girl Ella, but the icing on the cake (or the cookie) after all my hard work, persistence, and stepping over fear and obstacles was receiving an email stating I was chosen by Girls Scouts of Greater Chicago and Northwest Indiana to receive their "Smart Cookie" award. This award honors women who are changing the rules of the game and serving as role models for the next generation of girls and youth. I had no plans to rest on those laurels. The award was a continued call to action for me.

When 2017 came I dove headfirst into speaking engagements. Again, I had to navigate a new business, and I thought, *why do I keep doing this to myself?* I did what I have always done: I asked questions and learned everything I could about the speaking industry. One of my first steps was to join eSpeakers, an online speaking platform, which I read was good for new speakers. There I acquired many good leads but also the attention of the Washington Speakers Bureau, who became my speaking agent and still is today.

The speaking engagements started to come in with my first paid engagement from girls' clothing retailer, Justice, a subsidiary of Ascena Retail Group in Columbus, Ohio, in June 2017. This was followed by speaking engagements throughout the country at the University of Iowa, TMC, a division of C.H. Robinson, She Leads Media, Motorola Solutions, Indiana University, Integrating Woman Leaders Foundation, Indiana Conference for Women, American Association of University Women, Girl's Empowerment Network, Empowering Girls for Life and so many more including a highlight: a TEDx Talk.

I spoke to groups from as small as twenty people to as large as 2,000 people on the importance of empowering women and girls and my entrepreneurial journey. I loved speaking in front of a crowd, and I loved all the questions and interacting with others. I was doing my part to help spread the Go! Go! Sports Girls message. I wanted to keep the momentum of 2016, so the market would be ready for the relaunch in 2018.

Once during a large conference where I was the key-note speaker, my nerves started to take over. In addition to being on stage, I would be projected on two jumbotrons as well. This kind of freaked me out, and right before I went on stage, self-doubt started to flood my brain: *Who am I again? Why do they want me to speak?* I closed my eyes, took a deep breath, and did my best Amy Cuddy power pose. I pulled my shoulders back, lifted my chin, and said to myself, "You've got this. Your message is more import-ant than your nerves—do this for girls and women, who deserve more." Now before I go on any stage, I always tell myself those important words.

Karen was the lead on the Go! Go! Sports Girls brand. We had a great relationship, worked well together, she understood my vision and mission, and I had complete confidence in her ability. So, when Jazwares decided to pull all the Read & Plays off Walmart shelves and Amazon, I trusted that decision and supported their goal to launch a line of hard-body (plastic) Go! Go! Sports Girls dolls at Toy Fair in 2018. I felt even better about that decision when Lisa and her team at Walmart gave their approval, since hard-body dolls sell better in the mass retail space.

Karen and her team developed four-inch hard-body prototype dolls that embodied everything I loved about the original plush dolls. Each doll was dressed in her sports uniform, gym shoes, and hair in ponytails with a headband. They took on a new adorable yet fierce expres-sion, which is hard to get right on a doll. There were no high heels, crop tops, make up, belly button rings or big hair. They captured exactly what I envisioned in a way that represented girls as they really are right now: strong, smart, and adventurous.

Jazwares created a new sporty logo, brand colors that weren't pink or purple, packaging that showed action, and sports accessories. They were keeping with my vision and breaking every gender stereotype trope, and I loved it. They met with large publishing companies to publish the books and had the interest of Nickelodeon to create content and shows. Their brand strategy was to launch an aspirational brand directed to today's girl that would fill the current void in the toy market and break the mold of the "pink aisle." The voice of the brand would encompass girl-power messaging that shouted fierce, strong, brave, smart, and empowered. They were working hard for the big launch in February 2018.

My big dream was happening. Finally happening. I was proud and excited to see where the Go! Go! Sports Girls were headed. Everything was falling into place... and just as it was, the world was becoming more and more alert to the subjugation of women through the #MeToo Movement. If there was ever a time to launch a doll that championed girl empowerment, that time was now.

CHAPTER 30

#METOO

"Never doubt that a small group of thoughtful
committed individuals can change the world. In fact,
it's the only thing that ever has."
– Margaret Mead

There is so much misconception in our culture about the word *feminism*. Feminism has been associated with strong, forceful, and angry women, and our society continues to push back against strong, forceful—and especially—angry women. There is fear associated with feminism. Fear of overturning traditions, religious beliefs, established gender roles, and control. Feminism by definition means: the theory of the political, economic, and social equality of the sexes. It's about equal rights and equal access to opportunities.

In 2016, Hillary Rodham Clinton was the first US woman to secure the Democratic presidential nomination, and I was confident women were rising, and equality was happening. As an advocate for women and girls, I was shocked when our country elected a president with a misogynistic past. My mission became more important, and I was not alone. Women did not want to go backwards and bonded together to make their voices heard. The power of women became a force to be reckoned with.

On January 21, The Women's March became the largest single-day protest in US history. A new statue named Fearless Girl was installed on Wall Street in New York. *Wonder Woman* became the highest-grossing Superhero origin film. A record number of women ran for political office, and the #MeToo movement went global.[1]

The #MeToo movement was inspired by activist Tarana Burke in 2006, but the hashtag began circulating and multiplying on Thursday, October 5, 2017 after a breaking story in the *New York Times* by reporters Jodi Kantor and Megan Twohey, revealing their two-year investigation into the sexual misdeeds of film producer, Harvey Weinstein. This led to a fury over the insidious ways women have been and are mistreated and the shame and silence it provokes in them.

The day after the #MeToo story broke was the kind of day I'd usually sneak away to walk my dog or take a bike ride—but I stayed glued to my computer because my inbox was filled with comments, questions, and articles from women I knew and didn't know, sharing their stories and wanting to know more about the #MeToo movement. A door opened for women to feel a certain 'safety in numbers' to share their personal stories. Stories they thought were exclusive to them and too embarrassing to talk about, either because of what happened or because they were afraid they would be held responsible or not believed. Those were the same thoughts I had in eighth grade.

---

1   Lauren Alexis Fisher, "The 15 Best Moments for Women in 2017" (Harper's Bazaar, December 20, 2017), https://www.harpersbazaar. com/culture/features/g14456966/best-moments-for-women-2017/.

That evening, Steve and I had dinner with two other couples on the patio of our favorite local spot, and the #MeToo conversation continued, but this time it included men.

My two female friends and I started to share our personal sexual harassment stories—the ones that happened before I entered the workforce. I told the story of walking into a crowded fraternity party with my boyfriend, a friend, and her boyfriend. I was walking behind my friend's boyfriend when he quickly turned around and full on grabbed my breasts with both hands. I think he thought no one would notice because it was so crowded, and I would keep quiet, except I didn't. I screamed loudly and hauled off and punched him in the chest. Everyone around us saw what happened. A few guys rushed me out of the party while my friend's boyfriend stayed, and I was told to calm down. I don't know what, if anything, was said to the guy who violated me, but the message for me was that I was overreacting.

Another friend shared her story of walking into a college party and being trapped in a room with three guys who threw her down on the bed. Her girlfriends heard her screams and rescued her. She never reported it to the police or university. I shared my peeping Tom story while in my thirties, and my stalker story that lasted over one year while I was in high school. The story of a guy at a large dinner party who offered me one hundred dollars if he could watch me eat a banana. We shared butt grabbing stories, crotch grabbing stories, and name calling stories. This went on and on and on as our husbands listened and looked at us in a state of shock.

Steve's hand was covering his mouth, and his eyes were opened wide.

"Are you okay?" I asked.

"All this has happened to all of you?"

In unison, my friends and I replied, "YES!"

Then, very gingerly, not wanting the answer he knew I was about to deliver, asked, "Has anything like this ever happened to Grace?"

I nodded my head.

He wanted to know why I had never told him about my stories or Grace's stories. At this point I felt time stop. Should I tell him the other story? The one I had never told him? That I was date raped at the age of seventeen and vowed to myself to never tell a soul? Do I find the courage to tell him and my closest and dearest friends now and break my promise with myself? Time caught up with me, and I kept my promise. I went on to explain to him that women share harassment stories with other women because we understand. It's a safe zone, and we won't be judged.

Years later, I did tell Steve, and again he asked why I had never told him, anyone, or the authorities. He knew some of my stories, including the peeping Tom and high school stalker stories, but I told him I was afraid no one would believe me and that I would be questioned why I had put myself in a position where something like this could happen. I didn't want to be judged. I didn't want to carry this with me publicly for the rest of my life, and I didn't want to be labeled. This was additional pain on top of the pain I had already suffered, and I couldn't bear it. I was part of the 63 percent of women who never report sexual assault because of fear of repercussions. Women are taught early on not to make waves, and I easily fell into this trope.

Unfortunately, most cultures are set up to silence women, and once the #MeToo movement started, some men became vocal about the vocal women and their fear of being falsely accused. President Trump said, "It is a very scary time for young men in America." Some men went to an extreme approach and abided by the "Mike Pence Rule." Vice President Pence has said he "avoids any appearance of impropriety by never dining or having drinks alone with a woman other than his wife."[2] Sure, this is a way to avoid accusations, but it unfairly limits opportunities for women, and, well, it's ridiculous.

Let's flip it. What if I said to a potential male employee that my husband had to join us for our meeting to avoid any possible sexual assault or harassment on his part. The man would rightfully be insulted, and in turn every woman should rightfully be insulted by men who abide by the "Mike Pence Rule."

False accusations of sexual assault are extremely rare, but let's look at it statistically. According to the National Sexual Violence Resource Center, "the majority of sexual assaults, an estimated 63 percent, are never reported to police and of the 37 percent that are reported, between 2 and 10 percent are false reports,[3] which often get

2   Joanna L. Grossman, "Vice President Pence's 'Never Dine Alone with a Woman' Rule Isn't Honorable. It's Probably Illegal." (Vox, March 31, 2017), https://www.vox.com/the-big-idea/2017/3/31/15132730/pence-women-alone-rule-graham-discrimination.

3   *False Reporting, National Sexual Violence Resource Center (2012).*

labeled as such because of inconsistent definitions, protocols, and guidelines for reporting."[4] This percentage is also similar rate to false reports of other crimes. So put another way, even the small percentage of false reports might be dismissed, not because they didn't actually happen, but because of technicalities. In fact, men have a 1 in 467,000 chance of being falsely accused of rape; whereas 1 in 5 women and 1 in 71 men have experienced rape or attempted rape in their lifetimes.[5] To put it into even more perspective, you have a 1 in 15,300 chance of being struck by lightning.[6] You are more likely to be struck by lightning than falsely accused of rape.

No one should be falsely accused, but that doesn't diminish the much larger percentage of women who *are* being sexually assaulted and harassed. Women need to share their stories, and good men need to listen and help.

Let's also flip and put an end to the phrase "violence against women and girls." Why? Because the perpetrator is completely taken out of the conversation, and the sole focus is put on the victim. For example, for female rape survivors, 98.1 percent of perpetrators are men. For male rape survivors, 93 percent of perpetrators are men. [7] "Male violence" is a more appropriate term.

---

4   *False Reporting, National Sexual Violence Resource Center (2012).*

5   Valerie Jarrett, "A Renewed Call to Action to End Rape and Sexual Assault" (National Archives and Records Administration, January 22, 2014), https://obamawhitehouse.archives.gov/blog/2014/01/22/renewed-call-action-end-rape-and-sexual-assault.

6   NOAA US Department of Commerce, "How Dangerous Is Lightning?" (National Weather Service, March 12, 2019), https://www.weather.gov/safety/lightning-odds.

7   Michele C. Black et al., *National Intimate Partner and Sexual Violence Survey: 2010 Summary Report, 2010.*

In March 2021 in south London, the disappearance of a young woman led police to advise women to stay at home and be extra vigilant. Sounds reasonable, right, because that's what women are used to doing: protecting ourselves. Now let's flip it as a woman in London did, suggesting it would be better to impose a curfew on men instead of women to stop them from committing crimes. By the amount of hate mail she received, many men did not like or take kindly to her suggestion. We need to start framing "male violence" as problems for men and women to solve rather than a danger women need to avoid.

On a gorgeous summer evening, my husband and I were walking along the beautiful and quiet Illinois Prairie Path. Roe versus Wade had just been overturned by the Supreme Court, and I was feeling the weight of the world and needed to talk. My fear was, and still is, that there will be a rise of sexual assault and violence against women—a rise in "male violence."

I asked Steve, "Have you ever been afraid of running, walking, or biking alone?"

He responded, "No, have you?"

I said, "All the time. I always have to be careful." I went on to ask, "You know how we have always told Grace to be careful while running by herself and have advised her to run in populated areas? Do you know why we are telling her to be careful? Do you know why I have to be careful? Do you know why all women have to be careful? It's not because of a rabid racoon or lost dogs! It's men. We have to be careful of men. We were telling Grace to be careful of men who may hurt her." So, I will say it again: MEN, you need to help to stop "male violence."

I have heard this response before: "But not all men are violent." While I agree—I also know that not all sharks eat people—I'm not willing to jump into shark-infested waters.

You may be wondering, how can a sports doll change anything? Where does a doll fit into the #MeToo Movement? When I imagine a young girl left to engage in creative play with a sexy-looking doll (most likely marketed and sold by a company led by men), I wonder if that could very well be her first #MeToo moment. The assault is in the message: "Your value is in your appearance, and by the way, this is the standard with which you need to conform."

But if you give a girl a doll, a t-shirt, a science kit, and media that reinforces that she is strong, smart, brave—that she is valued for her abilities, not her appearance—it could potentially have a ripple effect in her life. And what about boys who grow up with this alternative narrative rather than seeing girls sit on the sidelines or as the supporting character. That matters too. Would a girl's confidence continue to grow throughout her childhood and not peak at the age of nine? Would she believe that her gender can do anything beyond the age of five? Would equal pay become a non-issue? Would the number of sexual assaults and harassments decrease? Would we see gender quality in our lifetime?

How do we know it will change anything until we try? It's like the butterfly wing causing a hurricane. It's a minor adjustment in our culture that could have magnanimous effects. But some people are caught up in the belief that a toy is just a toy, or a doll is just a doll, but what if a toy can change culture?

I am thankful for the #MeToo Movement for giving women a platform and a louder voice. It has impacted our country and countries around the world. The timing was perfect to launch the new line of Go! Go! Sports Girls. Our country was ready for a girl empowerment brand.

CHAPTER 31

SOFT LAUNCH HARD FALL

"Women belong in all places
where decisions are being made."
— Ruth Bader Ginsburg

"It's going to be a soft launch," Karen said. She had called me in January 2018 with an update on how Jazwares was proceeding with the Go! Go! Sports Girls redesign.

"A what?" I asked.

"A soft launch at Toy Fair. To see the type of response we get from buyers. We're moving the full launch to February 2019," Karen explained. A soft launch is a pre-view of a product with little to no marketing to gather customer feedback prior to an official release.

I had done my part with the speaking engagements, and I was eager to have the product on the market. I ended all my presentations saying, "In 2018 Jazwares will release the new line of Go! Go! Sports Girls dolls, and together our goal is to inspire and empower girls through-out the world."

A soft launch was like someone telling me to step back or speak more quietly. I didn't want a soft launch; I wanted a strong, bold, *loud* launch. This landed a direct hit on my optimism. I had to rally against my disappointment: I sold the brand to Jazwares, and I needed to trust their expertise. As a seasoned toy company, they knew what they were doing, and I needed to trust their judgement. They wanted to go about this correctly. I needed to be patient.

The week after Toy Fair 2018, I checked in with Karen.

"How did the buyers respond to the new Go! Go! Sports Girls design?"

"They only showed two dolls," she said, "so there wasn't much attention."

This seemed odd to me. What was going on? I started to get nervous. They were going to launch the brand, right?

I expressed my concerns to Karen, and she reassured me they were moving forward with the brand. She believed in the brand, and I believed in her. I had to keep my faith in Jazwares and keep my focus on public speaking. But doubt crept into my self-talk about needing to be patient and optimistic — and of course Jazwares was moving forward with the brand. My gut was telling me something different: that they were not as enthusiastic about the brand as they were eighteen months ago.

But what changed? Why were they backing off on a girl empowerment product after the second and largest Women's March had just taken place only a month prior, in January 2018, bringing 2.5 million people to Washington DC and some 4 million to cities around the world?[1] The US Women's National Soccer Team was making world headline news for their fierce fight for equal pay. The #MeToo Movement was at its peak, spark-

---

1   Leanna Garfield and Zoe Ettinger, "14 of the Biggest Marches and Protests in American History" (Business Insider, June 1, 2020), https://www.businessinsider.com/largest-marches-us-history-2017-1.

ing social change that could significantly shape our world going forward. We were in the midst of the third wave of feminism. Our social climate was perfect to reintroduce the Go! Go! Sports Girls. I had experienced this hesitation over and over in the toy industry for ten years, but if there was ever a time the world was ready for a doll that broke stereotypes, that time was now.

Throughout the year, I asked Karen multiple times, "Are you sure they are moving forward with the Go! Go! Sports Girls?" As much as I tried to talk myself into feeling confident, I had doubt. She always replied, "Yes." I knew Karen was a champion of the brand, but I also knew she wasn't the only person involved in the decision making at Jazwares.

In November, Karen emailed me to let me know that Jazwares hired a new senior vice president of marketing, George, and a new vice president of marketing, Jorge, and they wanted to schedule a phone meeting in December to review the relaunch of the brand. She also brought up a concern; George and Jorge were struggling with a strategy, the right blueprint to launch a girl empowerment brand. She said it would be beneficial if I could help explain a strong strategy to pitch to them.

I couldn't believe what I was hearing, but my gut had been right all along. I told Karen I didn't understand what the struggle was to launch a girl empowerment brand. Why is it any different than other brands? Why would the implementation of a girl empowerment brand be difficult? As a strong feminist, Karen understood. She was advocating for the brand as were the other women on the Go! Go! Sports Girls team, but as hard as they were pushing, they felt pushback from two men. I felt like I was back walking into the toy store looking for a science kit for my kids and being annoyed there was a boy science aisle and a girl science aisle. Now, like then, I followed directions and didn't make waves but was boiling beneath the surface.

I was determined to make this work and convince George and Jorge that together we could make Go! Go! Sports Girls a household name and inspire and empower girls throughout the world. This felt like my last shot, and until now, I had never felt more was at stake for the future of the Go! Go! Sports Girls. I wasn't about to take this on alone. I considered the people who had supported me through this journey, and I looked for others to join my pack.

Through my friend Brenda, I met a dynamic woman, Cherri Prince, who was the Executive Vice President of Seed Strategy, a full-service marketing firm located in Cincinnati, Ohio. When she was in Chicago we met for breakfast and immediately hit it off. I called Cherri for her help and guidance. She agreed, and over the next two weeks helped me, Kara, and Karen prepare a detailed PowerPoint to present to George and Jorge during our meeting.

The presentation highlighted the opportunity in the marketplace for a line of toys dedicated to girl empowerment. That the Go! Go! Sports Girls encourage and validate a girl's identity and supports her drive to be strong, smart, and brave, the very tools girls need to become confident leaders of tomorrow. It pointed out in the age of tech and endless toy choices; dolls remain in the top five most popular gifts for girls.

It explained our buyers. Mothers who control 85 percent of household purchases. Women who are experiencing a cultural awakening and want a product like Go! Go! Sports Girls to give to their daughters, nieces, and other girls in their life, a doll that represents who they are now, that uplifts their identity as active and athletic, and affirms their strong mind and body.

And to the retailers, the presentation explained how this new line of dolls and books provides a much-needed choice to their customers. The Go! Go! Sports Girls not only align with girl's interest in sports but also the emerging values girls are seeking today—agency and self-determination.

My goal from the start was to launch a socially responsible brand, but Jazwares was more concerned about revenue, so I did comparisons with other doll brands. I pointed out that American Girl had a vision to teach American history and created a world that generated $451.5 million in sales in 2017. Groovy Girls provided an alternative to Barbie and offered individuality with $100 million in annual sales. And Barbie addressed social norms in the 1960s and became a classic toy with almost $1 billion in annual sales.

I researched and read for weeks. I spoke to educators and researchers and gathered articles. I read an essay on Mattel and the designer Ruth Handler's creation of Barbie. A sentence made me pause. I read it again and again.

*In **1959, Barbie** was marketed with current social roles of a woman. **Mattel** represented the doll to mothers as a tool to make each girl a **"poised little lady,"** a social* *desire. **Ruth Handler**, the designer, believed through **this adult** figure that girls could dream her dreams, a concept **unheard** of in the **1950s**.*

Wait! This is what I did, but some sixty years later. I did a comparison.

*In **2009, the Go! Go! Sports Girls** were marketed with current social roles of a woman. **Dream Big Toy Company** represented the doll to mothers as a tool to validate and encourage girls as "**strong, smart and adventurous**" while placing an emphasis on **what a girl's body could do versus appearance**, a social desire. **Jodi Norgaard**, the designer, believed through **these childlike** figures that girls could stay true to herself and dream her dreams, a concept **desired** in the **2000s**.*

Like Ruth Handler, I was social listening and taking a cultural pulse. I was confident we could create a movement, a brave new world for girls that represents who they are right now. A world that focuses on what their minds and bodies can do versus what their bodies look like. We had all angles covered, and it was a powerful and compelling PowerPoint. I was ready to go.

CHAPTER 32

BOUND BY UNCONSCIOUS BIAS

"Look at what this country accomplished only
using half of its talent, just think of the potential for
the future…we, by some rather stupid decisions,
essentially put half of our talent on the sidelines."
– *Warren Buffett*

As an entrepreneur and mother, I have worked hard, juggled a lot, and I've been dedicated to both my work and my family. When Steve and I would attend social or business functions where we would meet new people, there were two common interactions: (1) people would ask if I worked, or (2) they wouldn't ask at all with the assumption that I neither worked nor had a career prior to children.

If I were asked if I worked, my response was either to say I own Basket Expression, I'm raising three kids, I own Dream Big Toy Company, or a combination of two, depending on the time of my life. If I answered with simply business owner, I can't tell you how many times men and women responded, "What a cute little business."

I wanted to scream.

But I avoided confrontation, remained polite, and responded, "It's not a *cute* little business, and it's not easy running a business and raising kids."

Then I figured out a way to leave the conversation. I can guarantee my husband, who has his own law practice, and male entrepreneurs in general, have never been told they have a "cute little business" or ever said, "it's not easy juggling a business and kids."

A few years ago, Steve and I were having dinner with good friends, and one friend asked me, "How's your little TED Talk coming along?"

I was a deer in headlights. He's my good friend, and I was processing how to calmly explain that my TED Talk wasn't little. Well, I didn't need to. His wife immediately swooped in like a badass angel.

"Little? Did you just call her TED Talk *little*? What if you came home after a big presentation at work, and I asked you, 'How'd your little presentation go?' You would be pissed!"

He knew he was wrong and looked at me with sincerity and apologized.

Women are also guilty of minimalizing their own achievements and referring to their accomplishments as "little." I've heard this often from women, and I am quick to point out that the "little" needs to be permanently dropped from their vocabulary, and there is nothing little about their achievements. However, women are expected to be modest, and when we challenge the modesty norms and talk about our personal accomplishments, we can feel discomfort. Women do a great job promoting other women, but to promote ourselves seems awkward. As

New York Senator Kirsten Gillibrand said, "The guy on my left thinks he's awesome, and so does the one on my right. If I don't think I am and promote it, I'm behind."

These are just a couple of examples of subtle messages that minimized my efforts. This wasn't just happening to me; this happens every day to women throughout the world. Whether explicitly or implicitly, such subversion seems harmless enough, but when I think of this happening collectively to women in general, I could see how it worked "to keep women in their place." Calling my TED Talk "little" was not so far removed from telling me girls prefer fashion dolls. Such comments—even those made by people we hold dear—undermine a woman's confidence in her identity, power, and agency.

Some people refer to such comments as a micro-inequity: a subtle comment or action, often sent unconsciously or consciously, that devalues, discourages, or marginalizes the recipient. This is different than, but similar to, a micro-aggression: a comment or action that subtly and often unconsciously or unintentionally expresses a prejudiced attitude toward a member of a marginalized group. They are verbal, nonverbal, and environmental slights, snubs, or insults that are deeply rooted in our culture, often go unnoticed by the offender, and have a hidden meaning.

Gendered microaggressions children often hear include, "You run like a girl," "You throw like a girl," "Don't cry like a girl," "Boys don't cry," and "Man up." These terms suggest girls are weak, and boys are strong. As activist and co-founder of A Call to Men, Tony Porter said, "If it would destroy him to be called a girl, what are we then teaching him about girls?" These phrases not only affect how men treat women or how boys treat girls, but how women treat women and girls treat girls.

Dr. Audrey Nelson, gender communication specialist, writes, "It's important to remember that everyone has biases and that most bias stereotypes do not come from a place of bad intent. It's a deep-seated, unconscious stereotype that's been formed in our brains through years of different influences we were exposed to and that we often had no control over."[1]

Unfortunately, our unconscious bias impacts our actions, and to change this, we need to make the unconscious, conscious. We all are guilty of unconscious bias and make mistakes; it's about improving our behavior after receiving critical feedback and speaking up when we recognize unconscious bias in others. My friend who corrected her husband did just that. We need more women and men to find courage to swoop in and be the badass angel for others who might not have the words to speak up for themselves; and when people's biases are pointed out, we need them to learn from and process that new perspective, and do better going forward, like her husband did in that situation.

A few years ago, I experienced the most remarkable and patronizing question I have received yet, and ironically, it was at an event prior to hearing Jodi Kantor and Megan Twohey speak about their new book *She Said: Breaking the Sexual Harassment Story That Helped Ignite a Movement*, so

---

1   Audrey Nelson, "How Unconscious Bias Impacts Women and Men" (Psychology Today, June 25, 2018), https://www.psychologytoday.com/us/blog/he-speaks-she-speaks/201806/how-unconscious-bias-impacts-women-and-men.

the majority of the room was filled with women. One of the hosts, a white male in his fifties, and I began talking. We exchanged details about our children and what we did for a living. He said he worked for a small boutique firm in Chicago that dealt with mergers and acquisitions. He then tilted his head, looked me square in the eyes, put his hand on my shoulder, and asked me, "Do you know what mergers and acquisitions mean?"

I wanted to say, "No, can you mansplain that to me?"

But I took a deep breath, gave a little chuckle and said, "Why yes, I do. My second business was acquired not too long ago by a large company."

Here was an opportunity for him to say: "My apologies, you obviously know about acquisitions. Please tell me more about your business."

But no, without skipping a beat, he proceeded to tell me all about mergers and acquisitions! Once I picked my jaw up off the floor, I found my way into a conversation with other women.

The term *mansplaining* was coined after Rebecca Solnit's essay, "Men Explain Things to Me: Facts Didn't Get in Their Way" was published online by TomDispatch in 2008. It struck a chord, and it quickly went viral. Solnit writes about a man at a party who said he had heard she had written some books. She begins to talk about her most recent book on Eadweard Muybridge when he cuts her off and asks with a smug look, "And have you heard about the very important Muybridge book that came out this year?" Solnit's friend, quickly responds, "That's her book." But he continues on, and her friend says three or four more times, "That's her book," before he finally gets a clue.[2]

Despite the steady stream of personal affronts, I know progress is being made to understand unconscious bias and change cultural attitudes and behaviors toward women and other oppressed groups. Those changes are not happening as fast as society demands, however, and I plan to keep pressing on toward more progress.

Now I was heading into a presentation where the future of Go! Go! Sports Girls was in the hands of two men, who more than likely harbored their own unconscious biases.

The phone call with George, Jorge, and Karen from Jazwares on December 17, 2018, started with introductions. Right away the energy and tone felt standoffish. I knew I had to do some convincing. There was little small talk, and I could tell Karen was nervous, but George and Jorge said they were looking forward to hearing more about the brand. I began to doubt my intuition and confidence in the presentation. I'll be honest, I feel more comfortable presenting the Go! Go! Sports Girls brand to women versus men. Over the years, I have found that most women understand the brand and connect with the importance for little girls to see aspirational and inspirational products. But when presenting to men, I typically receive that same response only half the time.

---

2 Rebecca Solnit, "Men Explain Things to Me; Facts Didn't Get in Their Way" (Common Dreams, December 21, 2022), https://www.commondreams.org/views/2008/04/13/men-explain-things-me-facts-didnt-get-their-way.

The presentation went smoothly with hardly any dialogue, so when I finished, I asked if there were questions.

"I'm concerned about launching a true girl empowerment product," Jorge said. "A few companies have tried to break into the girl empowerment arena and have failed."

I about did a spit-take!

"I've been a leader in the girl empowerment arena, especially when it comes to the toy industry, for almost ten years," I said. "There are only four true girl empowerment products on the market, and they haven't failed. People reach out to me or are referred to me often if they have a girl empowerment product idea. I would be surprised if I didn't know of a company or person with a girl empowerment product. Can you give me an example?'

"Hasbro tried to launch a girl empowerment product with Nerf Rebelle."

Thank goodness it was a phone meeting, so he didn't see my eyeroll! I took a breath to keep my composure.

"Hasbro wasn't successful with Nerf Rebelle because it fell into too many of the classic female tropes," I explained. "It advertises a "Pink Crush' bow, the packaging and product is painted with the epitome of girliness—pink and purple—and oddly, they changed the spelling of 'Rebel' to 'Rebelle.' On the packaging, the girls are posed, compared to the boys packaging where it shows action. They are trying to promote girl empowerment, but you can't fool people and just label something 'girl empowerment' when it falls into the same old flawed gender stereotyping."

He wasn't convinced. "Well, Disney has tried to break into the girl empowerment arena with the Disney Princesses, and they haven't had success."

Eyeroll again.

"There are eleven Disney Princesses, and many of the older films show women as weak and waiting to be rescued from their terrible lives by Prince Charming. Sure, in many of their more recent films the 'Princesses' break this mold with empowering characters. Disney is trying, and I give them credit, but at the end of the day it's still about a Princess."

He gave it one more shot and said, "What about Barbie?"

Really? This is how the toy industry views a girl empowerment product? Nerf Rebelle, Disney Princesses, and Barbie? This is the problem.

Taking another deep breath while rolling my eyes a third time, I remained calm.

"Mattel has tried many low-risk, half-hearted attempts to appeal to the girl empowerment market, most recently with their Role Models campaign. While I like this campaign, it's hard for Mattel to battle and break the Barbie stigma."

I proceeded to say, "I can appreciate you wanting to launch the brand correctly with a clear blueprint, and there is a correct way to do it. That requires being willing to let go of conventions and clichés that have come before, which the companies you brought up weren't willing to do. Girl empowerment done right requires breaking away from those conventions and clichés in a relevant and inspiring way. Authentically embracing girl empowerment requires taking a bold step forward out of the toy industry's comfort zone. That's how you lead a movement.

We can create a brave new world for girls. A world that represents who they are now—strong, smart, and brave."

George spoke up next.

"We are definitely moving forward with this brand. Let's schedule a meeting in person in January to go over further details. I would like you to come to Miami."

I felt my heart lift for the first time since the call began. But George wasn't done.

"The launch will most likely be pushed back a few months," he said.

I was glad he was part of the 50 percent of the men who understood. But I had the feeling Jorge didn't feel the same way.

CHAPTER 33

WHERE DOES IT END?

"Originality brings more bumps in the road,
yet it leaves us with more happiness
and a greater sense of meaning."
– *Adam Grant*

After we ended the conference call, I immediately called Karen back.

"What'd you think?" I asked. I wasn't thrilled with further delay, but it was a concession I was willing to live with if they stayed committed to relaunch the line.

"It went great," Karen assured me. "I'm glad they are moving forward with the brand."

I detected skepticism in her voice, but I questioned myself again. Was I the one being skeptical?

A week later Karen sent me an email with our next meeting date: January 15, 2019. After waiting more than two years, I only had one more month to wait. I was cautiously optimistic, and to prevent myself from thinking otherwise, I distracted myself with holiday cheer.

I rang in the New Year and felt 2019 would be the time for Go! Go! Sports Girls to receive broad acceptance. This year the dolls turned ten, and I had worked hard not only to get them on retail shelves but also in challenging the status quo that had kept them off the shelves in the first place.

Take 2014, when *Sports Illustrated* released their swimsuit issue with Barbie on the cover. I called all the major networks and emailed as many producers as I could find asking them to have me on their show. I said they needed a different point of view because this celebration of Barbie on the cover of *Sports Illustrated* was not good for our girls or our boys. They all turned me down, but I was proud I didn't let the moment go uncontested. Every time anything like that happened within our social culture, I did my best to respond. As entrepreneur and best-selling author Seth Godin said, "Either you defend the status quo, or you invent the future." I was calling out gender stereotyping every time I saw it.

I have been persistent and know that even on a small scale, my efforts have contributed to helping solidify a movement. Was it wrong to believe I felt some entitlement that the Go! Go! Sports Girls would finally find a beloved place on retail toy shelves this year?

I didn't get far into 2019 before that bubble popped. On January 11, Karen emailed me to let me know our meeting was postponed once again due to George traveling to Hong Kong. She asked if we could meet in New York in mid-February at Toy Fair. I was disappointed in another delay but accustomed to the disappointment. I had to be willing to wait. I had no choice.

Right after our meeting was postponed, I decided to email Laura Zebersky, the president. She was the ultimate decision maker and the person who initially decided to acquire the Go! Go! Sports Girls. I sent her a compelling letter pointing out the strengths of the Go! Go! Sports Girls brand and the potential to create a brave new world for girls and encouraged her to lead and push what's possible. I pointed out that she was a strong woman, and we could inspire young girls to be like her. I was hanging on by a thread and giving it my all.

And then that last thread broke.

On February 4, Karen called. Her voice was sad, and I knew what was coming. It wasn't easy for her.

"Jodi, I'm sorry, but we're not moving forward with the brand. George, Jorge, and Laura continue to struggle on how to launch a girl empowerment brand."

In my public speaking events, I mentioned how Karen and Jazwares were my important moment number three and always said enthusiastically at the end, "In 2019, together we will empower girls throughout the world!"

What was I going to say now? My story couldn't end here. My mission was too important. I had worked hard for more than a decade to get this far. What would it take for the top toy executives to believe girls deserved more?

After so many disappointments, this particular one felt damaging and felt final. I didn't see how the Go! Go! Sports Girls brand could recover. While part of me believed this should be a sign to put an end to this dream, deep down I didn't want this to be true. What I knew to be true was that my product didn't fit the toy industry mold. Go! Go! Sports Girls required more than an auto-pilot marketing plan. Jazwares was right; this wasn't just another doll line; this was a girl empowerment brand and deserved a launch that would lead a movement.

Because Jazwares never moved forward with the brand — in fact, let it stall out for two and a half years — I asked Karen and Laura to return the intellectual property to me, so I could look for another partner. Jazwares agreed, and in 2019 returned the intellectual property at no charge, knowing I had already paid a price for lost momentum. I guess you could say it was the best breakup possible.

Before Jazwares had officially returned the rights, and with their permission, I was contacting other toy and publishing companies throughout the world trying to find a new home for the brand. I didn't want to get back into manufacturing, so I knew finding a partner was the only route.

Mattel invited me to their headquarters to present to their team, but then backed out, saying they decided fashion was their focus. Other large toy companies showed interest, but no one was willing to pull the trigger and commit. I continued to hear comments from toy industry and publishing professionals riddled with gender stereotypes. "Girls who play sports don't play with dolls." "Generally, kids who are active don't read." "Boys don't read books about girls." I began to wonder if we had made any progress in the ten years since I started on this path because the assumptions toy buyers were making about kids were as false as they were then.

Months went by, and I still couldn't find a company willing to take on my brand. Sure, everyone believed what I had was much needed on toy shelves, but they weren't willing to be the ones to make it happen. I have learned that in our culture we talk a good talk about the importance of empowering women and girls but cower and hesitate when it comes to implementation. That's when I began to realize my journey in the toy industry was about more than a doll.

As I continued to get speaking requests, the feedback after every presentation was overwhelming: people agreed the toy industry's approach was flawed; gendered and sexualized toys were harmful; that toy companies were disconnected with the needs of children for the sake of profits and inertia; and when consumers knew better, they wanted better. That's when I decided to write this book. More people needed to understand the significance toys had on our children's development and identity, and that too many toy companies were pushing their own agendas on consumers.

When I announced I was writing this book, I was surprised to receive a few negative and angry comments. One toy industry professional wrote on my LinkedIn page, "Why do we tell girls to be masculine and boys to be feminine? It's not good for society." Another man responded, "HOORAY FOR GENDER STEREOTYPES!"

A man I know approached me at a party after hearing about my book and the news of Jazwares returning the intellectual property to me and said bombastically with subtle joy, "I knew your brand would never be successful!"

These comments still rattle and confuse me, but they also fuel my fire. I'm *not* giving up. I have taken on this battle and will continue to fight for equality for women and girls.

By the end of 2019 I continued to tell my story, not really knowing if I had an ending.

CHAPTER 34

MY STORY

"When you get into a tight place and everything
goes against you, till it seems as though you could
not hang on a minute longer, never give up then, for
that is just the place and time that the tide will turn."
– *Harriet Beecher Stowe*

I was born in Blue Island, Illinois, a south suburb of Chicago in 1964, during the second wave of the Women's Rights Movement, the year Title VII Civil Rights Act was passed, prohibiting employment discrimination on the basis of sex as well as race, religion, and national origin, and the year Dr. Martin Luther King Jr. was awarded the Nobel Peace Prize for his nonviolent resistance to racial prejudice in America.

Change was happening, and my mother believed in it all. My mother was twenty-two years old when I was born. She was the youngest of four girls raised in the south suburbs of Chicago. My mother was ambitious, a good student, and admired for her hard work. Sadly, her father made it clear he would never pay for any of his daughters to go to college because…they were girls, and they should find a husband.

She had few choices and has always been bitter and resentful about this, and I don't blame her. She was determined to give me and my sister more choices and always told us, "College is not optional; the option is which college."

Later in life, when my sister and I were in grade school, she went to college and earned her degree in nursing. I have always been proud of her for her accomplishment and wonder if she had been given the opportunity to attend college at eighteen, would she have become a doctor? My guess is yes.

She had to fight for her spot in life. She had to fight for her education. She had to fight to be heard when she had so much to offer.

My father also had to fight, but his fight was different. His fight was to escape poverty. He was the middle child of three boys born and raised in Terre Haute, Indiana to an Italian immigrant father and a strong-willed Irish mother. Unlike my mother's parents, his mother was determined to have her boys go to college. They didn't have much money, so hard work was their only option. My father worked multiple jobs and played multiple sports. He always said, "I am great at nothing but good at everything." I always disagreed, knowing he played baseball and ran track to much acclaim at Indiana State University.

My father was twenty-eight years old when I was born and had a wonderful and fulfilling career as a health teacher and coach of multiple sports. He started his teaching career at Bremen High School in Midlothian, Illinois, and in 2006, he was invited to the class of 1956's fifty-year class reunion, the first class he ever taught. During the reunion, and to his surprise, his former students gave him a standing ovation, and he was thanked by many for his kindness and guidance. I don't know if he has ever felt so touched or surprised, but indeed it was well-deserved.

During the weekends, when my mom was working, my dad would bring my sister and me to basketball games or track-and-field meets. I have fond memories of being a gym rat and a track rat surrounded by young people working hard and having fun. No doubt this played a huge influence on my love for and participation in sports.

I have always wondered if my mother had a brother, would he have been encouraged to go to college, and if my father had a sister, would she have been encouraged to find a husband and not attend college?

My parents met in 1962; nine months later they were married, and nine months after that I was born. My sister, Karen, was born three years later.

We lived in a progressive time in the late 1960s and early 1970s. Cultural change was happening, and I saw this progression and change in my family dynamics when my mom went to college and began her nursing career, and my dad took on household chores including laundry, grocery shopping, and cooking. I was proud of both of my parents for stepping out of their gender norms, but I don't think they saw it that way at the time. They were just trying to hold it all together.

My parent's relationship was rocky from the start. They were equals in our household but not equals in society, which ultimately led to their divorce after twenty-eight years of marriage.

Both were kind, smart, charming people. My father was recognized in our culture and rewarded, but my mother's same skill, talent, and character was not. But she was beautiful, which was highly recognized and rewarded, and she used it to her advantage. She knew the power of beauty and how that power could open doors and provide opportunities in ways a woman's intellect rarely would.

She often told me when I did poorly on a test or a paper, "Don't worry, honey, you will get by on your looks." I saw how this could both be true and how I didn't want this to be true. This may have been true for my mother, but I wouldn't believe this for myself. I was certain, by the time I became an adult, society would treat women differently.

But that didn't come to pass, and in fact, I saw that message play out in obvious and subversive ways throughout my life. I was so tired of it but never felt like I had any agency to change the narrative until I encountered Lovely Lola. Ever since I have fought like hell to be heard.

CHAPTER 35

NOW WHAT?

"Scream so that one day a hundred years from
now another sister will not have to dry her tears
wondering where in history she lost her voice."
– Sikh poet Jasmin Kaur

I began 2020 with my usual optimism even though I still didn't have any interest from potential buyers. I figured the new year couldn't get any worse.

There is nothing like a shelter-in-place order during a world pandemic to keep you at home, in front of your computer, writing your story.

There is nothing like social unrest to keep you focused on the need for equality.

There is nothing like a contentious presidential election and subsequent insurrection to keep you supporting advocates and leadership that fight on behalf of women and girls.

In the turbulent year that was 2020, the Geena Davis Institute on Gender in Media reported on how harmful stereotypes still hinder girls, boys, and their parents. It found that parents still encouraged sons to do sports or STEM activities, while daughters were offered dressing up or baking. But if that's all the toy industry offers, what choice do they have?

According to Gina Rippon, a neurobiologist and author of *The Gendered Brain*, toys offer training opportunities. "If girls aren't playing with Lego or other construction toys, they aren't developing the spatial skills that will help them in later life. If dolls are being pushed on girls but not boys, then boys are missing out on nurturing skills." [1]

My role in changing attitudes and policies regarding gender stereotypes in the toy industry was to provide a sports-themed doll in the toy industry. Yet 2020 would have been an easy year to give up on finding a partner for the Go! Go! Sports Girls. Trust me, I thought about it, but I couldn't. I was committed to the social change business and fighting for girls, women, and overall gender equality. I had to find a way to move forward because progress toward gender equality was looking bleak. Between the combined impact of social conflict and unrest, extreme weather events, and COVID-19, there was a greater and immediate effect on women and girls worldwide being deprived of basic needs such as food security, essential health services, and education. This also led to a "shadow" pandemic to COVID-19: the reverse progress in expanding women's rights and opportunities led to an increase in violence against women and girls. [2] Or let's call a spade a

1   Helen Russell, "Lego to Remove Gender Bias from Its Toys after Findings of Child Survey" (The Guardian, October 10, 2021), https://www.theguardian.com/lifeandstyle/2021/oct/11/lego-to-remove-gender-bias-after-survey-shows-impact-on-children-stereotypes.

2   "What Does Gender Equality Look like Today?" (UN Women, October 26, 2021), https://www.unwomen.org/en/news/stories/2021/10/feature-what-does-gender-equality-look-like-today#:~:text=A%20new%20global%20analysis%20of,burdens%20of%20unpaid%20care%20work.

spade—an increase in male violence. Then total abortion bans criminalized performing the procedure quickly took place in thirteen states after the overturning of Roe versus Wade in 2022, and many pregnant women with medical emergencies were denied or delayed medical treatment due to anti-abortion legislation.

There are many areas that women and girls need help and advocacy, but I needed to focus on my area of expertise. When I considered what I could do in that turbulent moment, I reached out to Laurel Wider, founder of Wonder Crew. We teamed up to spearhead and lead the diversity, equity, and inclusion committee for the Toy Association. Until then no such committee existed for the organization. We set out to build awareness and provide best practices for creating diversity within toy companies' missions, workforce, products, and content development. At the same time, we set our eyes on something bigger.

Shortly after President Joe Biden took office in 2021, he established the new White House Gender Policy Council and named Julissa Reynoso and Jennifer Klein as the council's leaders. Laurel and I saw an opportunity to create change on a larger scale, so we reached out to Jennifer asking if there was an opportunity for us to help. Within hours Jennifer replied, "We would love to work together." Laurel and I were collaborating with the White House again, and our first task was to create a proposal outlining our vision and suggested solutions.

We arranged meetings with leaders and key change-makers throughout the world who were working hard to create gender equality including Let Toys Be Toys and the Fawcett Society both located in the UK and the

French Embassy. France is a leader in combating gender stereotypes from an early age. They recognize the need to advance women in the workforce and are committed to fight against the prejudices that can divert them beginning in childhood. France and England were making great progress, more than the US, but ironically both countries were looking to the US for leadership, and sadly, we have nothing concrete to provide.

Five weeks later, Laurel and I presented to the Gender Policy Council our proposal on Equal Play: Elevating Toy and Media Industry Standards to Empower ALL Children to Explore and Dream Without Limits. We pointed out various industry disparities, marketing, and representation issues in toys and media as well as research informed suggested solutions including legislation and policy, education, advocacy programs, campaigns, research, and a White House conference similar to the one held in 2016.

Around this same time is when Laurel and I secured funding from the Toy Association to hire the Geena Davis Institute on Gender in Media to conduct the study on whether gender norms are reinforced in toys and toy advertising and marketing. A study like this had never been done before, and the White House Gender Policy Council was interested in reviewing the report.

This is the study I referred to in chapter one. This is the study the Toy Association decided not to release. Laurel and I did not accept their decision without further discussion. We offered suggestions on how to release the findings without using company or brand names, since offending their financial supporters was one of the issues concerning the Toy Association.

Two months passed without a response. Laurel and I were losing hope. I felt similar to how I did in my journey with Go! Go! Sports Girls and the toy industry; I would get so far, so close, and then tumble back to the beginning because someone got cold feet. I had a strong feeling this was happening again.

But to my surprise, in late March 2023, Laurel and I received an email from The Toy Association stating, "In the interest of time and certainly gauging White House interest, we can take our name off the research and allow you/Laurel to do as you wish with the research (ensuring companies are not listed within the report.) I hope this helps to move a larger initiative to fund further research. Thank you both for your extraordinary work and commitment!"

Ultimately, I'm grateful The Toy Association opted against withholding the report, and in December 2023 the *Equal Play* report was finally and officially released to the public. This initial report is a huge leap in educating children's toy, media, retail, and publishing industries—and consumers—on the cognitive, social, emotional, and creative benefits of non-gendered play.

CHAPTER 36

A DOOR OPENS

"If you believe it'll work out,
you'll see opportunities. If you don't believe it'll
work out, you'll see obstacles."
— *Wayne Dyer*

The First Lady requests the pleasure of your company at an event celebrating Girls Leading Change to be held at The White House on Wednesday, October 11, 2023 at three o'clock

This is the email I received on October 3, 2023. I was honored to be invited to the first-ever Girls Leading Change event and be part of the White House Gender Policy Council's programing. In honor of International Day of the Girl, First Lady Jill Biden would celebrate fifteen young women leaders leading change and shaping a brighter future.

I was familiar with the procedure of entering the White House, but this event was different than the meeting I attended in 2016. This was a celebration. A quartet played at the entrance of the East Wing. Flowers lined the halls and formally dressed military escorts directed attendees to the East Room, which was buzzing with young girls from organizations such as Girls on the Run and Girl Scouts of the USA. Attendees also included several members of Congress and other women changemakers.

Jennifer Klein, director of the Gender Policy Council kicked off the event and introduced First Lady Jill Biden, who said about the honorees: "These young women are protecting and preserving the earth, writing and sharing stories that change minds, and turning their pain into purpose. Together they represent the potential of young people across the country, and it is my hope that others can learn from the power of their innovation, strength and hope."

Press secretary Karine Jean-Pierre closed the event stating, "Fearlessness is our superpower. As women and young women, we need to be fearless to bulldoze through the obstacles that are placed in front of us every day. We must fearlessly fight for our rights and our freedoms and the rights and freedoms of all women." It was an inspiring presentation, making clear girls are a powerful force in the fight for gender equality whose ability and potential should not be overlooked.

The celebration continued with a reception as White House staff served cupcakes and lemonade in wine glasses on silver platters. I finally had the opportunity to meet in person my contacts at the Gender Policy Council, including Senior Advisor, Morgan Mohr. I asked if other toy industry leaders were at the event.

Morgan introduced me to two people from the C-suite of a major toy company. We were the only changemakers from the toy industry at the event, so I was curious about their work.

They shared their belief that play is essential for personal growth, development, and happiness, and their recent commitment to a girl-centered leadership development initiative of the United Nations Foundation, and an in-house program to promote innovations for girls.

They were speaking my language!

I gave them a quick overview of Go! Go! Sports Girls and told them the brand was acquired in 2016 by Jazwares, but quickly added, "They returned the brand to me, so it's available if you're interested."

They wanted to set up a call to learn more. And just like that my hope was renewed.

But unlike Jazwares, this wasn't going to happen in five minutes. In fact, as I write this chapter in August 2024, the conversation with this toy company continues. If I've learned anything in this business, it's patience. What's different now is the "why" has become more compelling for toy companies. And the support continued to grow as the weeks and months of 2024 passed. I felt as if the universe was spoon-feeding me new information about the explosive growth in women's sports, thus, supporting the existence of my brand and reasons to acquire it:

- The WNBA opened the 2024 season with their highest attendance.[1]

- The 2024 NCAA women's basketball championship had viewership of 18.7 million compared to the men's championship of 14.8 million.[2]

- Business management consulting firm, Deloitte, predicted that 2024 revenue generated by women's elite sports will surpass $1

1   WNBA Opens 2024 Season with Highest Attendance in 26 Years and Most-Watched Games Ever on National TV (WNBA, June 10, 2024), https://www.wnba.com/news/tip-off-2024-success-breakdown

2   The Magic of March: Men's and women's tournaments highlight continued growth, impact of college basketball (NCAA, April 12, 2024) https://www.ncaa.org/news/2024/4/12/media-center-the-magic-of-march-mens-and-womens-tournaments-highlight-continued-growth-impact-of-college-basketball

billion for the first time, 300% higher than predicted in 2021.[3]

- The growing number of companies making efforts to increase their investments in women's sports, including: Google, Nike, Ally Financial, Mastercard, Coca-Cola, Morgan Stanley, and Delta.[4]

- A WNBA press release reporting unprecedented growth, with more than half of all WNBA games selling out and merchandise transactions up 756% from last year.[5]

- An article from Front Office Sports, *"Women's Sports Merch Is a $4 Billion Market, but Supply Isn't Meeting Demand,"* stating that media and commerce company, Togethxr, started by four athletes: Alex Morgan, Chloe Kim, Simone Manuel, and Sue Bird, generated $3 million in revenue in seven months on its $45 "Everyone Watches Women's Sports" t-shirt.[6]

---

3   Women's elite sports: Breaking the billion-dollar barrier (Deloitte, November 28, 2023) https://www2.deloitte.com/us/en/insights/industry/technology/technology-media-and-telecom-predictions/2024/tmt-predictions-professional-womens-sports-revenue.html

4   Women's Sports See Rise In Popularity and Investment (Sports Business Journal, August 2023), https://www.sportsbusinessjournal.com/Native/Isos/2023/August.aspx

5   WNBA Opens 2024 Season with Highest Attendance in 26 Years and Most-Watched Games Ever on National TV (WNBA, June 10, 2024) https://www.wnba.com/news/tip-off-2024-success-breakdown

6   Women's Sports Merch Is a $4 Billion Market, but Supply Isn't Meeting Demand (Front Office Sports, July 16, 2024) https://frontofficesports.com/womens-sports-merchandise-market-4-billion/

- A report titled *Rep Her: Revealing the Unmet Demand for Women's Sports Merchandise.*[7]

This "unmet demand" has existed for years—certainly existed that fateful day I walked into my local toy store shopping for a birthday gift with my 9-year-old daughter. I am certain this unmet demand for "Women's Sports Merchandise" trickles down to "Girls Sports Merchandise," and includes toys. No doubt, the same women who want to buy sports merchandise are the same women who would purchase a sports doll for the young girls in their lives.

Some 15 years ago, I believed the Go! Go! Sports Girls was a major business opportunity, in the same way corporate analysts are now seeing the potential. I'm not someone who believes I'm infallible. I don't believe I'm right all the time. But I *know* I am right about this.

From day one the Go! Go! Sports Girls have been well received, but as you have read so far, that support was grounded more in "this is the right thing to do for empowering girls" than in "this is the right thing to do for the company's bottom line." What's happening now, that hasn't happened before, is the acknowledgement that investing in girls and women in sports isn't risky, it's good for business. In the arc of this long journey of mine, that is a massive shift.

---

7   Rep Her: Revealing the Unmet Demand for Women's Sports Merchandise (Klarna and Sports Innovation Lab, June 26, 2024) https://static1.squarespace.com/static/630a5e16691e080692afb271 /t/667b28e1b39cc82598965346/1719347426020/RepHer_Sports+ Innovation+Lab+Fan+Project+X+Klarna.pdf

And yet, I still don't know if my brand will be acquired, even if the time has come for the intersection of sports play and immersive toy play. I still believe in this brand whole-heartedly and I'm as optimistic as I've ever been. But even if the Go! Go! Sports Girls don't ultimately return to toy shelves, they will have paved the path for better choices in children's play. I know in my heart these dolls have made an impact on creating a blueprint for the toy industry to progress and reflect who children are and who they want to become.

CHAPTER 37

HOW WE MOVE FORWARD

> "There are days where I get discouraged. There are moments where I am deeply, deeply disappointed. And, yes, there have been moments where I have stopped and said, 'Is this worth it anymore?' And every time I do that, I lick my wounds for a while, sometimes I cry. And then I say, 'Ok, let's fight.'"
>
> – *Justice Sonia Sotomayor*

Women have been fighting for the basic human right of equality for almost 200 years and, according to the World Economic Forum's 2022 Global Gender Gap Report, we have 130 years of hard work still to go to reach equality. It shouldn't be this difficult. It shouldn't take this long. What's more alarming, according to the United Nation's 2023 Breaking Down Gender Biases report, gender equality has gone into reverse.[1]

The head of the UN Human Development Report Office, Pedro Conceicao, expressed his shock at the magnitude of bias toward women and the lack of progress. The biases result in barriers for women in politics, business, and work as well as the stripping away of their rights and human rights violations. He stated, "It was also a period

---

1   "2023 Gender Social Norms Index (GSNI): Breaking down gender biases: Shifting social norms towards gender equality," (UNDP: Human Development Reports, 2023).

in which we saw, for example, the #MeToo movement and a lot of visibility to the very shocking ways in which these bias norms affect women."[2]

Heidi Stöckl, a professor specializing in gender-based violence at Ludwig Maximilians University of Munich said, "We have experienced a serious backlash and roll-back of women's rights, most notably in Afghanistan but also in the western world with the election of Donald Trump or in South Korea, where an anti-feminist president was elected recently. What makes me hopeful is that, in the majority, the younger part of the population clearly resents this backlash and is striving for an equal society."

Andrea Simon, director of the End Violence Against Women Coalition said, "These views persist because of social and cultural norms that devalue women and reinforce men's power, control and feelings of entitlement, as well as promoting beliefs that trivialize and normalize violence against women and even blame victims for their own abuse. It is these attitudes that can drive violent acts and behaviors and we can only truly prevent this violence by shifting these attitudes."[3]

How can we help the younger generation strive for equality? How can we shift social relationships and power dynamic attitudes? How can we reshape social and

2   Kaamil Ahmed, "Nine out of 10 People Are Biased against Women, Says 'alarming' UN Report" (The Guardian, June 12, 2023), https://www.theguardian.com/global-development/2023/jun/12/nine-out-of-10-people-are-biased-against-women-says-alarming-un-report.

3   Kaamil Ahmed, "Nine out of 10 People Are Biased against Women, Says 'alarming' UN Report" (The Guardian, June 12, 2023), https://www.theguardian.com/global-development/2023/jun/12/nine-out-of-10-people-are-biased-against-women-says-alarming-un-report.

cultural norms that devalue women? Where can we fast track gender equality? I say look to when it starts. I'm sounding the siren that gender inequality doesn't begin in our teens and twenties; it begins the moment a child can hold a toy or book or watch a screen.

As hard as I've fought to get a sports doll on the market, as much as I've heard from parents how they want better options for their daughters, sexy dolls prevail with few alternatives and, in some ways, are even more bold in their sexuality. For instance, in 2020, children who own MGA Entertainment's L.O.L. Surprise! dolls may have discovered a water feature, which wasn't publicly promoted by the company. When some of the dolls were dipped in cold water, sexy lingerie appeared. One even had a devil tail on her backside, and another reveals "Caution" over her private area and shackles on her wrists.

How could anyone in the toy industry sign off on that?

In response to the criticism, an MGA spokesperson said in a press release, "L.O.L. Surprise! is a fashion-forward doll brand designed to be fun and expressive. We work very hard to be a brand that listens and adapts to our fans' requests."[4]

I'd like to know who, exactly, they're listening to. I don't know a single parent who wants their little girls playing with a doll that's dressed for a night of S&M.

Toys have become far too sexualized and gendered to be innocent playthings. In a world where women and

---

4   Christopher Zara, "L.O.L. Surprise! Doll Maker Finally Responds to Those Viral Ice-Water Videos" (Fast Company, August 15, 2020), https://www.fastcompany.com/90540562/l-o-l-surprise-doll-maker-finally-responds-to-those-viral-ice-water-videos.

girls are climbing out of the pits of sexism and stereotypes and fighting back on issues of pay equity, representation, and sexual harassment, it's time to take our case to younger and younger stakeholders and hold toy companies accountable for their treatment—I'd even say harassment—of young girls.

Another example is the Fail Fix Dolls by Moose Toys, which comes with a removable 'failed face' with failed hair and smudged makeup. The goal is for children to be the style savior by transforming the dolls to help fix the beauty fail, reinforcing the stereotype that girls and women are most valued for their attractiveness. If they don't look pretty, they are failing.

In 2022, the Children's Advertising Review Unit (CARU) determined Moose Toys and Fail Fix Dolls failed to comply with guidelines that advertising should not portray or encourage negative social stereotyping, prejudice, or discrimination. "CARU determined that the Fail Fix advertisements characterize a girl with imperfect makeup and messy hair as a failure and worthy of public embarrassment, which is likely to perpetuate negative and harmful stereotypes about girls, specifically that they must look perfect to feel good about themselves. They concluded that the messages placed undue pressure on girls to conform to artificial standards of beauty and perfection to see themselves as valued."[5] In response, Moose Toys discontinued the line.

---

5   Abby Hills, "Moose Toys Discontinues Fail Fix Dolls Advertising to Comply with CARU" (BBB National Programs, August 10, 2022), https://bbbprograms.org/media-center/dd/moose-toys-fail-fix-dolls#:~:-text=McLean%2C%20VA%20%E2%80%93%20August%20 10%2C,a%20provision%20stating%20that%20advertising.

Children's Advertising Review Unit (CARU) is a program run by the Better Business Bureau to encourage industries toward self-regulation. According to its website, this particular program "helps companies comply with laws and guidelines that protect children under age 13 from deceptive or inappropriate advertising and ensure that, in an online environment, children's data is collected and handled responsibly." Those "laws and guidelines" refer to the Children's Online Privacy Protection Act (COPPA).

Consumers buy toys in good faith assuming they are appropriate for children and believe toy makers have children's best interest at heart. But gender stereotypes remain prevalent in today's toys, and our complacency feeds inequities and stereotypes. As consumers, the work begins with us because accepting what's on the toy shelves is a huge part of the problem. We have to speak up.

Eight-year-old Annie Rose Goldman did just that when she noticed Rey was missing from Hasbro's *Star Wars* version of Monopoly. She wrote, "How could you leave out Rey in Star Wars Monopoly? Without Rey, there is no Force! It awakens in her!" Raising the consciousness of toy companies through personal pleas is part of the battle to break gender stereotypes in media and toys. We have to call out toy companies when they are too lazy to go beyond formulaic and stereotyped products to provide better choices for our children.

WHAT CONSUMERS CAN DO TO ADVOCATE FOR HEALTHY TOYS

A shift in consumer attitudes puts more pressure on retail leadership, which will lead to the toy industry stepping up with innovative and new products—and create that new blueprint the toy industry so desperately needs. Here are ways you can do your part.

- **Rewire your brain to recognize gender stereotypes and inequalities.**
    - Where our attention goes our energy goes, so throw your attention into education, observation, and cultural conversations (check out the resources to get started at the end of the book). Known as neuroplasticity, the brain can grow and learn to function in new ways.

- **Once you know better, practice doing better.**
    - Talk about the unfairness of stereotypes and inequalities with children in your life.
    - Be mindful of unconscious bias in language and expectations. For example, complimenting girls on their appearance and boys for their strength.
    - Encourage children to speak up, share their thoughts, opinions, feelings, and to lead. Especially girls, so they don't start losing confidence at the age of eight.

- ○ Embrace and nurture confidence and assertiveness in girls and empathy and compassion in boys.

- ○ Champion sensitive children. Research shows kids who are highly sensitive show more creativity, awareness, openness, empathy, and deep thinking. They are the future leaders we need.[6]

- **Demand representation and products free of reinforcing stereotypes from the toy, publishing, retail, advertising, and media industries.**

  - ○ Buy products that nurture a child's interest and ambition; avoid products that pigeonhole children into thinking they need to behave or look a certain way. Money talks.

  - ○ Let companies know when they have it wrong. Reach out to them directly or file a complaint with the Children's Advertising Review Unit (CARU) online at www.bbbprograms.org or by email, infocaru@pppnp.org.

---

6   Jenn Granneman, "Kids Who Do These 12 Things Have 'highly Sensitive' Brains-Why Parenting Experts Say It's an 'Advantage'" (CNBC, March 8, 2023), https://www.cnbc.com/2023/03/04/parenting-experts-signs-your-kid-has-a-highly-sensitive-brain-why-neuroscientists-says-its-an-advantage.html.

WHAT THE TOY INDUSTRY CAN DO TO ADVOCATE FOR HEALTHY TOYS

This work doesn't fall entirely on the shoulders of consumers. The toy industry can and should do better. I obviously can't change the toy industry on my own, but I do have some ideas of where it can start.

- Product design commitments from toy manufactures to undertake developing toys that promote racial diversity, gender diversity, and break stereotypes.

- Doll body proportion standards. Similar to the mandatory set of safety rules toymakers are required to follow, dolls should be held to safe proportion standards.

- Policies similar to those that protect children from products that may cause physical harm.

- Thematic rating system similar to television, movie, and video game ratings to bring attention to various content, themes, or play patterns.

- Awards given to toy brands that challenge and fight against gender stereotypes.

- Training for buyers and toy industry professionals about the impact of toys, suggestions for improvement, and guidelines for children's age and interests rather than gender.

- Retail restructuring, so stores are organized by interest, not separated by gender.

- Advertising that rejects rigid gendered social norms or an outdated gender binary.[7]

- Marketing strategies that disrupt gender stereotypes including colors, music, and language.

- Promotion of awareness campaigns on social networks.

- Equal representation of female and male protagonist characters in publishing and media. We need female characters who are physically active and actually speak. And we need children's publishing companies to let go of the foolish and antiquated notion that boys won't read about girls and active girls don't read books.

- Risk-taking by toy, publishing, retail, advertising, and media companies to create the change required to allow children to be represented as they are instead of telling them who they should be.

KEEP GIRLS IN SPORTS

I must advocate for getting girls and keeping girls in sports. Ultimately, I still believe giving a budding or passionate little athlete a sports doll can go a long way to validate her interest and bolster her resolve to stay in her game. As

---

[7]   "Ban on Harmful Gender Stereotypes in Ads Comes into Force" (Committee of Advertising Practice, June 14, 2019), https://www. asa.org.uk/news/ban-on-harmful-gender-stereotypes-in-ads-comes-into-force.html.

fellow changemaker Julie Kerwin said, "If you give a girl a different toy, she will tell a different story." For far too long the stories and dreams of women and girls have been sidelined and suppressed. What more can we do?

- Educate young girls on the lifelong benefits of sport and physical activity.

- Celebrate girls' strength, speed, and love for being active.

- Role model. Be active and be active with the girls in your life.

- Support women in coaching. There is a need for more women coaches and women in sports leadership positions.

- Support female athletes. At www.coachher.com, coaches of any gender can use a free tool, developed by The Tucker Center for Women and Girls in Sports, to learn more about how stereotypes and implicit bias can affect performance and lead to attrition.

- Attend and watch girls' and women's sporting events with girls *and* boys in your life.

WHAT WE ALL CAN DO TO ADVOCATE FOR GENDER EQUALITY

Finally, we must work together to fast-track gender equality. I have never thought or wanted to suggest that one gender is better, but in the race of life, the starting line for women is different and the track is longer. Here are a few suggestions on how we close the gap.

- **Support women and girls.**
  - ○ Studies show women who support women and have an inner circle of close female contacts are more successful in business and in life[8].
  - ○ Advocate for yourself and other women. This raises awareness of issues. And by raising the issue does not make you the issue.
  - ○ Use your voice, but when your voice or another woman's voice in the room isn't being heard or ignored, use the Amplification Strategy. When a woman makes a key point, another woman repeats it, making sure her thought, idea, and voice is being heard. This forces men in the room to recognize her contribution and diminishes the chance to claim the idea as their own.[9]
  - ○ Call out stereotypes, inequities, and challenge the status quo because this reinvents

8   Shelley Zalis, "Power of the Pack: Women Who Support Women Are More Successful" (Forbes, February 20, 2024), https://www.forbes.com/sites/shelleyzalis/2019/03/06/power-of-the-pack-women-who-support-women-are-more-successful/#:~:text=We%20need%20to%20reverse%20the,are%20more%20successful%20in%20business.

9   Juliet Eilperin, "White House Women Want to Be in the Room Where It Happens - The Washington Post" (The Washington Post, September 13, 2016), https://www.washingtonpost.com/news/powerpost/wp/2016/09/13/white-house-women-are-now-in-the-room-where-it-happens/.

the future. This isn't always easy and in turn you may be challenged. I have found three non-threatening questions that have helped me when I'm being challenged, and the ownership is put on the challenger.

- What do you mean by that?
- Tell me more about that?
- What are you afraid of?

○ Invest in women. According to the Bill & Melinda Gates Foundation, investing in women's economic power could grow the global economy an additional $10 trillion by 2030.[10]

- **Men need to help drive progress.**

○ Gender inequality is not just a woman's issue. Men need to be involved too. Women's participation at the table, whether it's business, socially, home life, politically, the results are more peaceful, prosperous, and profitable.[11] The table should reflect the society it represents. It's beneficial to all.

My daughter Grace, an avid soccer and tennis player in her youth and the one who inspired me to launch this

---

10   Melinda French Gates, "Melinda French Gates on How Leaders Can Boost Women's Economic Power" (Bill & Melinda Gates Foundation, October 4, 2023), https://www.gatesfoundation.org/ideas/articles/melinda-french-gates-how-leaders-boost-womens-economic-power.

11   United States Agency for International Development, Gender Equality and Women's Empowerment 2020 Policy.

line of dolls in 2008, is now taking on Chicago as a young professional, much like I did in my early twenties. Even though her days of playing with dolls are long behind her, I look back now, and I am grateful I fought hard to bring a product to market that seemed obvious and long overdue, helping girls lean into sports and into leadership.

Girls play sports and so should their dolls. I believe that, and I'll keep believing there is a place in the toy market for the Go! Go! Sports Girls. I don't know if I'll see gender equality in my lifetime, but I sure would like to see an end to gender stereotypes in media and toys.

I've learned nothing happens neatly on journeys, and there are no guarantees. I struggled, doubted, cried, picked myself up, and persisted because deep in my heart, in my soul, I know women and girls deserve more. I like to think that we are volcanos with untapped strength, wisdom, and power to move and create new mountains. A new blueprint.

That's how I want this story to end. As little girls experiment with how their bodies work when they play soccer, or learn to dance, or take their first swimming lessons, I want them to celebrate what their mind and body can do versus what their body looks like. I want them to express themselves in creative play that mirrors their interest in sports; to stay true to their strong body and smart mind; to create a beautiful new story—their own authentic story—that finalizes a new blueprint for gender equality.

I Was Told

By Jodi Bondi Norgaard

I was told I cannot be bold.
Be bold my dear, for you have much to offer.

I was told I cannot cry.
Shed tears my dear, for you are caring and kind.

I was told I cannot climb trees.
Climb high my dear, for there is so much to see.

I was told I cannot be strong.
Dig deep my dear, for you are fiercely brave.

I was told I cannot be loud.
Speak loudly my dear, for the world needs to hear
your voice.

I was told I cannot stand.
Stand tall my dear, for you were born to lead.

RESOURCES

Knowledge is Power

For a more completed list of updated resources, please visit www.jodibondinorgaard.com.

BOOKS

NON-FICTION

- *All in Her Head: The Truth and Lies Early Medicine Taught Us About Women's Bodies and Whit It Matters Today*, Elizabeth Comen
- *Bad Feminist: Essays*, Roxane Gay
- *Beauty Sick: How the Cultural Obsession with Appearance Hurts Girls and Women*, Renee Engeln
- *Becoming*, Michelle Obama
- *Be Fierce: Stop Harassment and Take Your Power Back*, Gretchen Carlson
- *Bernardine's Shanghai Salon*, Susan Blumberg-Kason
- *Boys & Sex: Young Men on Hookups, Love, Porn, Consent, and Navigating the New Masculinity*, Peggy Orenstein
- *Brandsplaining: Why Marketing Is (Still) Sexist and How to Fix It*, Jane Cunningham and Philippa Roberts
- *Cassandra Speaks: When Women Are the Storytellers, the Human Story Changes*, Elizabeth Lesser

- *Catch and Kill: Lies, Spies, and a Conspiracy to Protect Predators*, Ronan Farrow
- *Cinderella Ate My Daughter: Dispatches from the Front Lines of the New Girlie-Girl Culture*, Peggy Orenstein
- *The Confidence Code: The Science and Art of Self-Assurance — What Women Should Know*, Katty Kay and Claire Shipman
- *The Curse of the Good Girl: Raising Authentic Girls with Courage and Confidence*, Rachel Simmons
- *The Dance of the Dissident Daughter: A Woman's Journey from Christian Tradition to the Sacred Feminine*, Sue Monk Kidd
- *Down Girl: The Logic of Misogyny*, Kate Manne
- *Educated: A Memoir*, Tara Westover
- *Enough as She Is: How to Help Girls Move Beyond Impossible Standards of Success to Live Healthy, Happy, and Fulfilling Lives*, Rachel Simmons
- *Entitled: How Male Privilege Hurts Women*, Kate Manne
- *EVE: How the Female Body Drove 100 Million Years of Human Evolution*, Cat Bohannon
- *The Everyday Feminist: The Key to Sustainable Social Impact - Driving Movements We Need Now More Than Ever*, Latanya Mapp Frett
- *Feminasty: The Complicated Woman's Guide to Surviving the Patriarchy Without Drinking Herself to Death*, Erin Gibson
- *The Feminine Mystique*, Betty Friedan
- *Feminism is for Everyone: Passionate Politics*, Bell Hooks

- *A Fever in the Heartland: The Ku Klux Klan's Plot to Take Over America, and the Woman Who Stopped Them*, Timothy Egan
- *The Fix: Overcome the Invisible Barriers That Are Holding Women Back at Work*, Michelle King
- *Gender and Our Brains: How New Neuroscience Explodes the Myths of the Male and Female Minds*, Gina Rippon
- *Girls & Sex: Navigating the Complicated New Landscape*, Peggy Orenstein
- *Gloria Steinem: My Life on the Road*, Gloria Steinem
- *Good for a Girl: A Woman Running in a Man's World*, Lauren Fleshman
- *The Great Stewardess Rebellion: How Women Launched a Workplace Revolution at 30,000 Feet*, Nell McShane Wulfhart
- *Half the Sky: Turning Oppression into Opportunity for Women Worldwide*, Nicholas D. Kristof and Sheryl WuDunn
- *How to Be a Woman Online: Surviving Abuse and Harassment, and How to Fight Back*, Nina Jankowicz
- *I Am Malala: The Girl Who Stood Up for Education and Was Shot by the Taliban*, Malala Yousafzai
- *The Immortal Life of Henrietta Lacks*, Rebecca Skloot
- *Invisible Women: Data Bias in a World Designed for Men*, Caroline Criado Perez
- *Know My Name: A Memoir*, Chanel Miller
- *Mediocre: The Dangerous Legacy of White Male America*, Ijeoma Oluo

- *Men Explain Things to Me*, Rebecca Solnit
- *Men Who Hate Women: From Incels to Pickup Artists: The Truth About Extreme Misogyny and How It Affects Us All*, Laura Bates
- *The Moment of Lift: How Empowering Women Changes the World*, Melinda Gates
- *The Patriarchs: The Origins of Inequality*, Angela Saini
- *Radium Girls: The Dark Story of America's Shining Women*, Kate Moore
- *Rage Becomes Her: The Power of Women's Anger*, Soraya Chemaly
- *The Right to Sex: Feminism in the Twenty-First Century*, Amia Srinivasan
- *The Second Sex*, Simone de Beauvoir
- *She Said: Breaking the Sexual Harassment Story That Helped Ignite a Movement*, Jodi Kantor and Megan Twohey
- *The Sisterhood: The Secret History of Women at the CIA*, Liza Mundy
- *So Sexy So Soon: The New Sexualized Childhood and What Parents Can Do to Protect Their Kids*, Diane E. Levin and Jean Kilbourne
- *That's What She Said: What Men Need to Know (and Women Need to Tell Them) About Working Together*, Joanne Lipman
- *Untamed*, Glennon Doyle
- *We Should All Be Feminists*, Chimamanda Ngozi Adichie
- *Whose Story Is This? Old Conflicts, New Chapters*, Rebecca Solnit

- *WOLFPACK: How to Come Together, Unleash Our Power, and Change the Game*, Abby Wambach
- *Women & Power*, Mary Beard
- *Women Talking*, Miriam Toews
- *The Woman They Could Not Silence: One Woman, Her Incredible Fight for Freedom, and the Men Who Tried to Make Her Disappear (Ture Story of the Historical Battle for Women's and Mental Health Rights)*, Kate Moore
- *You Throw Like a Girl: The Blind Spot of Masculinity*, Don McPherson

FICTION AND HISTORICAL FICTION

- *The Alice Network*, Kate Quinn
- *Becoming Madam Secretary*, Stephanie Dray
- *Circe*, Madeline Miller
- *Code Name Helene*, Ariel Lawhon
- *The Diamond Eye*, Kate Quinn
- *The Dictionary of Lost Words*, Pip Williams
- *The First Ladies*, Marie Benedict and Victoria Christopher Murray
- *The Huntress: A Novel*, Kate Quinn
- *Lady Tan's Circle of Women*, Lisa See
- *Lessons in Chemistry: A Novel*, Bonnie Garmus
- *The Magnificent Lives of Marjorie Post*, Allison Pataki
- *The Other Einstein*, Marie Benedict
- *The Power*, Naomi Alderman
- *The Rose Code*, Kate Quinn
- *The Silence of the Girls: A Novel*, Pat Barker
- *When We Had Wings*, Ariel Lawhon

- *The Women*, Kristin Hannah

FOR CHILDREN/TEENS

- *Boys Will Be Human: A Get-Real Gut-Check Guide to Becoming the Strongest, Kindest, Bravest Person You Can Be*, Justin Baldoni
- *The Confidence Code for Girls: Taking Risks, Messing Up, and Becoming Your Amazingly Imperfect, Totally Powerful Self*, Katty Kay, Claire Shipman, and JillEllyn Riley
- *Express Yourself: A Teen Girl's Guide to Speaking Up and Being Who You Are*, Emily Roberts
- *Good Night Stories for Rebel Girls: 100 Tales of Extraordinary Women*, Francesca Cavallo and Elena Favilli
- *Heart of a Boy: Celebrating the Strength and Spirit of Boyhood*, Kate T. Parker
- *Raise Your Hand*, Alice Paul Tapper
- *A Smart Girl's Guide: Knowing What to Say*, Patti Kelley Criswell
- *Stand Tall, Molly Lou Melon*, Patty Lovell
- *Strong Is the New Pretty: A Celebration of Girls Being Themselves*, Kate T. Parker

PODCASTS

- *Feminist Book Club*, Rah Hernandez
- *The Fix, Michelle King*, Kelly Thomson, and Selina Suresh
- *Gender at Work*
- *The Guilty Feminist*, Deborah Frances-White

- *How to Talk to Kids About Anything*, Dr. Robyn Silverman
- *The Man Enough Podcast*, Justin Baldoni, Liz Plank, and Jamey Heath
- *Ms. Magazine – On the Issue*, Michele Goodwim
- *Next Question*, Katie Couric
- NPR, *Believed*, Lindsey Smith and Kate Wells
- *On the Issues*, Michele Goodwin
- *Ordinary Equality*, Kate Kelly and Jamia Wilson
- *Playing with Fire*, Shannon Watts
- *Scene on Radio*, Season 3, *MEN*, John Biewen and Celeste Headlee
- *Stuff Mom Never Told You*, Anney Reese and Samantha McVey
- *The Story of Woman*, Anna Stoecklein
- *UnF*uck Your Brain: Feminist Self-Help for Everyone*, Kara Loewentheil
- *United Bodies*, Kendall Ciesemier
- *Unladylike*, Cristen Conger
- *Unlocking Us*, Brene Brown
- *We Can Do Hard Things*, Glennon Doyle, Abby Wambach, and Amanda Doyle
- *Wiser Than Me*, Julia Louis-Dreyfus
- *Women's Liberation Radio News*
- *Women's Media Center*, Robin Morgan

TED TALKS

- *A Call to Men*, Tony Porter
- *How Online Abuse of Women Has Spiraled Out of Control*, Ashley Judd

- *Looks Aren't Everything. Believe Me, I'm a Model*, Cameron Russell
- *On Being a Woman and Diplomat*, Madeleine Albright
- *Tales of Passion*, Isabel Allende
- *This Tennis Icon Paved the Way for Women in Sports*, Billie Jean King
- *To Raise Brave Girls, Encourage Adventure*, Caroline Paul
- *We Should All Be Feminists*, Chimamanda Ngozi Adichie
- *Why I Believe the Mistreatment of Women Is the Number One Human Rights Abuse*, Jimmy Carter
- *Why We Have Too Few Women Leaders*, Sheryl Sandberg

DOCUMENTARIES

- *Fair Play*
- *Game On: Women Can Coach*
- *The Hunting Ground*
- *The Illusionists*
- *The Invisible War*
- *The Janes*
- *Killing Us Softly*
- *The Mask You Live In*
- *Miss Americana*
- *Miss Representation*
- *RBG*

ACKNOWLEDGMENTS

I couldn't have written this book without my dear friend, editor, and Go! Go! Sports Girls author, Kara Douglass Thom. Your support and friendship is invaluable and I thank you from the bottom of my heart.

To the best literary agent I could ever have imagined. Thank you Elizabeth Copps for believing in me. To Debra Englander, it has been an honor to work with you, Caitlin Burdette, and so many others at Post Hill Press.

Thank you to everyone who shared their own stories and knowledge of the sports and toy industries with me—over email, phone calls, Zoom, text. Your input within these pages reassures me I'm not alone on this journey and that momentum is building. Change is coming.

To my pack, thank you for your support and encouragement over the last two decades. It has energized me and kept me going. Finally, a giant thank you to my kids and husband, my favorite people in the world.

ABOUT THE AUTHOR

Jodi Bondi Norgaard is an entrepreneur, author, keynote speaker, TEDx speaker, and a feminist activist pushing media and retail to do a better job portraying women and girls beyond stereotypes. She is the creator of the award-winning Go! Go! Sports Girls line of dolls, books, and apps, encouraging healthy and active play over beauty and body image.

She has been featured on national media including the *Today* show, *The Real Story with Gretchen Carlson*, *Forbes*, *Parents*, and *Huffington Post*. Jodi is a contributor to *Ms.* magazine.

As a recognized thought leader, she was asked by the Biden-Harris administration to be part of the groundbreaking Gender Policy Council and collaborates on issues as it relates to children's toys, content, and publishing.

Jodi is a proud graduate of Indiana University with a BA in psychology.